EL INCA
GARCILASO DE LA VEGA

by

DONALD G. CASTANIEN

The Inca Garcilaso de la Vega (1539-1616), son of an Incan princess and a Spanish conquistador, holds a unique place in the history of American letters. His translation of León Hebreo's *Dialoghi d'amore* was the first book published in Spain by a mestizo.

His *La Florida del Inca* is an account of Hernando de Soto's exploration of the southeastern part of the United States. Based on the account given by one of de Soto's men, the *Florida* was designed to remind Spain that a valuable colony was about to be lost through neglect and lack of interest.

It was his *Royal Commentaries*, the history of his mother's people, that brought Garcilaso his greatest success and established him as an historian of the Incan civilization who must be taken into account by any later writers on the subject. A great hymn of praise for the glories of an empire destroyed by the Spaniards, its virtue lies not so much in its historical accuracy as in its reflection of the point of view of a true native of Peru. The *Royal Commentaries* are complemented by his last work, the *General History of Peru,* the story of the Spanish conquest and the subsequent civil wars.

Garcilaso de la Vega was a precursor of the twentieth-century novelists and poets who have sought to restore to the Indian something of his lost dignity.

EL INCA GARCILASO DE LA VEGA

TWAYNE'S WORLD AUTHORS SERIES

A Survey of the World's Literature

Sylvia E. Bowman, Indiana University

GENERAL EDITOR

PERU

John P. Dyson, Indiana University

EDITOR

El Inca Garcilaso de la Vega

(TWAS 61)

TWAYNE'S WORLD AUTHORS SERIES (TWAS)

*The purpose of TWAS is to survey the major writers
—novelists, dramatists, historians, poets, philosophers,
and critics—of the nations of the world. Among the
national literatures covered are those of Australia,
Canada, China, Eastern Europe, France, Germany,
Greece, Italy, Japan, Latin America, New Zealand,
Poland, Russia, Scandinavia, Spain, and the African
nations, as well as Hebrew, Yiddish, and Latin Classical literature. This survey is complemented by
Twayne's United States Authors Series and
English Authors Series.*

*The intent of each volume in these series is to present
a critical-analytical study of the works of the writer;
to include biographical and historical material that
may be necessary for understanding, appreciation,
and critical appraisal of the writer; and to present all
material in clear, concise English—but not to vitiate
the scholarly content of the work by doing so.*

El Inca Garcilaso de la Vega

By DONALD G. CASTANIEN

University of California, Davis

Twayne Publishers, Inc.   ::   New York

CARNEGIE LIBRARY
LIVINGSTONE COLLEGE
SALISBURY, N. C. 28144

Copyright © 1969 by Twayne Publishers, Inc.

All Rights Reserved

Library of Congress Catalog Card Number: 70-75875

MANUFACTURED IN THE UNITED STATES OF AMERICA

868.3
C346

Preface

The Inca Garcilaso de la Vega occupies a unique place in the history of Peruvian, Spanish-American, and Spanish letters. The son of a Spanish captain who took active part in the destruction of the Incan empire and of an Incan princess, the Inca Garcilaso carried with him to Spain a mixed heritage. After a childhood and early youth spent in Cuzco, he left his native land for Spain where he lived out a long life filled both with frustrated dreams and with great successes.

His was the first book published in Spain by a member of that new group, the mestizos, whose role in Spanish-American life was to become overwhelmingly important in many parts of America, especially after Spain's colonies established themselves as independent nations. The book, a translation rather than an original work, was followed by three others, all dealing with American themes and all intended as histories rather than as literary endeavors. However, the Inca Garcilaso displayed such excellent qualities as a writer that Menéndez y Pelayo, whose enthusiasm for Spanish-American letters was often less than overwhelming, referred to him as one of the two Spanish classics from America.[1] The other was Garcilaso's younger contemporary, the Mexican dramatist, Juan Ruiz de Alarcón.

It may be argued that biographical information on any writer is significant to the study of his creative work, or contrarily that biography has no bearing at all. In Garcilaso's case the biography has particular importance. Consideration of the years spent in Peru and in Spain will help clarify conditions which formed Garcilaso's attitudes toward the problems arising from Spain's conquest of the New World. Moreover, he invites the investigation of his life with the numerous autobiographical references in all his works except the first; the tone of his work is highly personal. He himself is present on nearly every page, unconcealed by any fictional disguise or cloak of anonymity. While he does offer considerable information about

[v]

73970

himself, for reasons of his own he is completely silent about some aspects of his life. This reticence has given rise to speculation about him particularly in regard to his years in Spain. As a result, certain sentimental, imaginative interpretations of his life have gained currency, fostered by his adoring admirers who have sought to make a romantic figure of him.

Recent investigations in Spanish archives have produced more objective and trustworthy information on the years he spent in Montilla and Córdoba. Archival records, however, leave many questions still unanswered. The information drawn from the archives has been available in Spanish for some time, but has not been generally known to English readers.

In considering the Inca's published works, a chapter has been devoted to each of them. His first book was a translation of a philosophical treatise, León Hebreo's *Dialoghi d'amore*, a sixteenth-century analysis of the nature of love. No attempt has been made to evaluate the significance of the ideas expressed in the work, primarily because it is not a statement of Garcilaso's original ideas but is rather a rendering into Spanish of the thought of another. The significance of the translation, so far as Garcilaso is concerned, lies more in his handling of literary Spanish than in the development of a philosophical theory.

In the case of the three original works on which Garcilaso's reputation mainly rests, an attempt has been made to assess them both for their literary and for their historical worth. His story of Hernando de Soto's expedition to Florida, *La Florida del Inca*, and his two-part history of the Incan empire and of its conquest by the Spaniards, the *Comentarios reales* and the *Historia general del Perú*, were intended by their author to be read as history. Since Garcilaso thought of himself as an historian, though a modest one, it has seemed fitting to consider his theories of history and his practices in writing it in order to place him in relation to the intellectual background of his own time. Garcilaso has been attacked because of inaccuracies in his work; he has been charged with excessive naiveté and gullibility in his acceptance of what was told him by his Indian relatives who were anxious to present the Incan cause in its best light. Today, comparatively few would defend Garcilaso as an absolutely trustworthy historian, but he cannot be ignored no matter what his shortcomings.

Final judgment on Garcilaso's accuracy as the recorder of Incan history must await more thorough investigations by archaeologists, anthropologists and linguists; no attempt has been made here to evaluate such scientific studies as have already been made relative to matters dealt with in Garcilaso's account of Incan and pre-Incan cultures. It has seemed more important to consider his historical writing in relation to the ideas of history that were current in the sixteenth and early seventeenth centuries.

The Inca Garcilaso de la Vega was a man who wrote with obvious bias, though he thought he was fair and impartial. He wrote with a definite purpose in mind; the intention here is to identify that purpose and to examine, as far as is possible, the causes that motivated his interpretation of Indian and Spanish life in Florida and Peru.

All translations are those of the author.

DONALD G. CASTANIEN

Contents

Chronology

1532   Francisco Pizarro enters Cajamarca.
1533   Execution of Atahualpa.
1534   Captain Sebastián Garcilaso de la Vega y Vargas arrives in Peru.
1537–
1554   Civil wars in Peru.
1539   Birth of Gómez Suárez de Figueroa, later known as the Inca Garcilaso de la Vega.
1541   Assassination of Francisco Pizarro.
1548   Battle of Sacsahuaman, execution of Gonzalo Pizarro.
1559   Death of Captain Sebastián Garcilaso de la Vega y Vargas.
1560   The Inca Garcilaso de la Vega leaves Peru for Spain.
1561   The Inca arrives in Montilla.
1569?–
1570   Garcilaso serves in the wars against the Moors in Granada.
1571   Death of Isabel Chimpu Ocllo, mother of the Inca.
1590   *Diálogos de amor* published.
1591   Garcilaso leaves Montilla for Córdoba.
1605   Garcilaso becomes majordomo of the Hospital of the Immaculate Conception of Our Lady in Córdoba; publication of *La Florida del Inca*.
1609   Publication of the first part of the *Comentarios reales*.
1616   Death of Garcilaso.
1617   Publication of the second part of the *Comentarios reales*, the *Historia general del Perú*.

CHAPTER 1

The Death of an Empire

A T Cajamarca, on the sixteenth day of November, 1532, the first
encounter between official representatives of two alien civiliza-
tions took place. Atahualpa, ruler of the great Incan empire, now
crumbling, had agreed, after an exchange of messages, to meet
Francisco Pizarro, a captain of the mighty Spanish empire at the
peak of its power and influence. Exactly what Atahualpa's notion
of the significance of the appearance of the strange white man was,
there is no way of knowing. What Pizarro's attitude toward the
Indian was is less obscure; he had embarked upon an expedition
with the permission and blessing of Charles V, King of Spain and
Holy Roman Emperor, and of his Council of the Indies for the
express purpose of exploring and conquering Peru, or New Castile.

Royal permission for the conquest was granted to Pizarro, the
illegitimate and illiterate son of a Spanish colonel of infantry, after
he had made explorations along the western coast of South America
and had collected evidence to show that the area was no less prom-
ising as a source of treasure than Mexico had been. With the priest
Hernando de Luque and the soldier Diego de Almagro, Pizarro lost
no time in preparing his expedition, consisting of three vessels, 180
men and twenty-seven horses, and sailed from Panama in January,
1531. His early forays inland produced treasure enough to encourage
him in his undertaking. Reinforcements which joined him at Puerto
Viejo helped him to establish himself on the island of Puná, at the
mouth of the Guayas River. He soon learned from native informers
that the Indian empire was torn by civil war between Atahualpa,
bastard son of the Inca Huayna Capac, and Huascar, his legitimate
heir. Armed with this information and supported by new arrivals
under the command of Hernando de Soto, later to become discoverer
of the Mississippi, Pizarro pushed on into the interior until he made
contact with the representatives of Atahualpa who, having taken

his half-brother Huascar prisoner, had established himself as ruler of the vast expanse of territory conquered by his father's people over the centuries.

Atahualpa's claim to the throne of the Incas was, according to tradition, a shaky one. The throne belonged to the eldest legitimate son of the emperor. Huayna Capac had proved himself a most able military leader in the conquest of the northern kingdom of Quito where he became enamored of a local princess and made her his concubine. Although Huayna Capac had a son Huascar by his sister-wife, it was Atahualpa, the descendant of the kings of Quito, whom he favored. When it came time to make his will and to provide for the succession, as was the custom among the Incas, Huayna Capac made the fatal mistake that assured dissension in the empire. Guided by a desire to express his affection for Atahualpa, he divided his lands, leaving Quito to Atahualpa and the rest of the empire to Huascar. Accounts of what happened immediately after the death of Huayna Capac, only a few years before the arrival of the Spaniards, vary considerably, but it is certain that Atahualpa succeeded in routing Huascar and his loyal army. By the time Pizarro and his men established contact with Atahualpa, he was in effect the ruler of the Incan empire and had placed upon his head the red *borla,* the Incan symbol of highest authority.

It is reported that before his death, Huayna Capac had received reports of white men along the coast and had predicted the fall of his empire to these mysterious strangers—a story that bears a strong resemblance to the Aztec legend of the coming of Quetzalcóatl. Strange portents were observed, again like the marvelous events that so shook the Aztec Moctezuma, and, if these accounts are to be credited, prepared the victorious Atahualpa to receive the Spaniards.

Arrangements were finally made for the meeting. The city of Cajamarca, emptied of its inhabitants, was left to the Spaniards who made it their headquarters. Atahualpa, with an army that far outnumbered the modest Spanish force, established his camp at some distance from the city. Pizarro, influenced perhaps by reports of Atahualpa's cunning and cruel efficiency, prepared to receive the Indian monarch in the city square by concealing his men in the buildings surrounding the square with orders not to show themselves until the command was given after the arrival of Atahualpa. They were to attack the Indians and take Atahualpa prisoner.

Atahualpa entered the apparently deserted city; when the plaza was filled with his attendants, Pizarro's chaplain Fray Vicente de Valverde appeared to explain the doctrines of Christianity, to urge Atahualpa to accept the true faith and to acknowledge himself a vassal of Charles V. It may be doubted that Atahualpa perfectly understood the discourse upon Christianity translated by the interpreter who had accompanied Pizarro from the coast. He did understand the suggestion that he should recognize the authority of the Spanish king. Atahualpa refused to deny his own religion and to admit Charles's superiority. When he questioned the source of Father Valverde's authority, the latter pointed to the Bible (some say it was a breviary) he was carrying. Atahualpa took the book, examined it briefly and then cast it to the ground.

The insult was too much; Pizarro gave the signal to attack, whereupon the Spaniards poured out of the buildings where they were concealed, and began a merciless slaughter of the Indians. The attempt to protect the person of Atahualpa was vain; the ruler of the great empire became the prisoner of the Spaniards.

Atahualpa was keen enough to observe that his captors were inordinately fond of gold and silver. Anxious to obtain his liberty, both because his imprisonment was an affront to his dignity and because it offered Huascar an opportunity to gain his own freedom and reestablish himself as ruler, Atahualpa offered to pay a princely ransom, a suggestion that the Spaniards found highly acceptable. Rumors reached Atahualpa that Huascar was indeed planning to recoup his fortunes and had offered an even greater sum to the Spaniards if they would rescue him. Atahualpa could ill afford the threat posed by Huascar's freedom; he had him murdered. Huascar is reported to have prophesied that his death would be avenged by the white men.

It may be doubted that concern for Huascar's death motivated the Spaniards to any considerable degree, but Atahualpa did not long survive his half-brother. He was tried by the Spaniards and found guilty of having murdered Huascar and, more important, of having stirred up insurrection among the Indians. He was sentenced to be burned alive in the public square, but because he accepted Christianity just before the execution, the supposedly more merciful garrote was substituted for the flames.

After the death of Atahualpa, Pizarro marched to the ancient capital of Cuzco where he set about organizing a government based upon the Spanish pattern. While engaged in this task, he received word of the arrival of another Spanish force led by the intrepid

Pedro de Alvarado, already famous because of his prodigious leap across a canal on the "Sad Night" when Cortés and his army escaped from the Aztec capital Tenochtitlán. Like many of his countrymen, Alvarado needed action; when the first excitement of the conquest of Mexico had worn off and after a relatively quiet period spent in Guatemala, he looked for other scenes of activity and was attracted by the promise of Peru. Suiting his interpretation of royal decrees to his own desires, he decided that Pizarro's claims did not include the kingdom of Quito; he therefore organized an expedition to exploit that territory and with a force of some five hundred men landed on the coast of northern South America.

Pizarro, whose ideas of his own rights did not correspond with those of Alvarado, sent his partner Diego de Almagro to challenge the intruder. By the time the two met, it was obvious that it was mutually advantageous to join forces. Alvarado had discovered that the kingdom of Quito did not offer all the rewards he had hoped for; Almagro and Pizarro could make good use of the additional strength offered by Alvarado's army.

While the Spanish conquest of Peru was by no means finished at the death of Atahualpa, that event meant that the political and military power of the ruling family was broken. That, along with the alliance between Pizarro and Alvarado, even though their combined forces were pitifully small compared with the vast numbers of the native population, assured that the Spaniards were in truth the masters of the country. The Indians, demoralized by the sudden collapse of their leadership, could not withstand the vigor and zeal of the successful Spaniards who began at once to build a new society, a new culture which drew upon Indian as well as Spanish tradition.[1] The new society produced a new people, the mestizos in whom the blood of their Indian mothers was combined with that of their Spanish fathers. Such a one was the Inca Garcilaso de la Vega.

CHAPTER 2

The Inca Garcilaso de la Vega: His Life

I *His Family*

GÓMEZ Suárez de Figueroa, or the Inca Garcilaso de la Vega, to give him the name he later adopted, was able to boast of distinguished ancestry on both sides of his family.[1] His father, Sebastián Garcilaso de la Vega y Vargas, was one of Alvarado's captains who elected to stay in Peru. Captain Garcilaso de la Vega was one of the nine children of Alonso de Hinestrosa de Vargas and of his wife Doña Blanca de Sotomayor Suárez de Figueroa, each of whose families had produced men famous in the history of Spanish arms and letters. On doña Blanca's side of the family, nearly every generation had produced a man whose exploits were recognized throughout Spain, commemorated in poetry and in history. The nearest in time to doña Blanca was her cousin, Garcilaso de la Vega, the Renaissance soldier-poet who, along with his friend, Juan Boscán, is generally credited with the renewal of Spanish poetry through the introduction of Italianate meters. The father of the poet, who bore the same name, made a career as soldier, courtier to the Catholic Kings and ambassador to Rome. More remotely in the family tree appear the names of Fernán Pérez de Guzmán and Pero López de Ayala, both of whom occupy prominent places in the history of medieval literature. No less significant for their contributions as soldiers and poets were the collateral connections, Admiral Diego Hurtado de Mendoza, Iñigo López de Mendoza, Marqués de Santillana, and Jorge Manrique.

The family of Alonso de Hinestrosa de Vargas could not boast of so many members whose names are found in every history of Spanish literature, but it was a family whose members left a glorious record with their heroic deeds in battle. Garci Pérez de Vargas accompanied Ferdinand I on his campaign against the Moors in Andalucia and his exploits during the battle for Seville were recorded by Fernán

Pérez de Guzmán in his *Loores de los claros varones de España.*
The sixteenth-century poet Garci Sánchez de Badajoz was a connection of the family.

Captain Sebastián Garcilaso de la Vega has left no evidence that
the literary life held any appeal for him. Rather, as for many of his
generation, it was the possibility of action, adventure and wealth
in the New World that attracted him. Exactly when he left Spain
for America is not known, but apparently about 1530 he was in
Guatemala where he joined Alvarado's expedition to Peru. Although
he arrived in Peru too late to become a member of the privileged
group known as the first conquerors, Captain Garcilaso de la Vega
soon became a person of consequence, having allied himself closely
with Francisco and Gonzalo Pizarro. As a reward for his services,
he was granted the forced labor of the Indians of Tapacari and was
identified beyond all question of doubt as a substantial member of
the ruling group in Peru.

At some time, probably in Cuzco, the Spanish captain yielded
to the charms of Chimpu Ocllo, a princess of the royal family, though
not in the direct line of succession. She was the niece of Huayna
Capac, the cousin of both Huascar and Atahualpa. Her father was
Huallpa Tupac, fourth son of the Inca Tupac Yupanqui and his wife,
Mama Ocllo. From the informal union of the aristocratic Spaniard
and the royal Indian princess, the future historian of the glories of
his mother's people and of their defeat by his father's people was
born April 12, 1539. Peru's first truly distinguished man of letters,
christened with the name of his Spanish great-grandfather, chose
later to be known as the Inca Garcilaso de la Vega, a name with
which he proudly advertised his double heritage.

II *His Youth in Cuzco*

The years of the Inca Garcilaso's childhood in Cuzco were
troubled ones.[2] From the very beginning of the conquest there was
dissension among the leaders. Each was driven by personal ambition;
each was suspicious of all the others, fearful lest a companion and
partner outmaneuver him and gain undue prominence in what was
originally a joint undertaking. Francisco Pizarro was a bold, determined man who did not always foresee the consequences of his
actions. His execution of Atahualpa aroused the ire of Hernando de
Soto who was absent at the time; de Soto maintained that the
emperor should have been tried before a proper court in Spain. But
de Soto's difference with Pizarro over the death of Atahualpa was

a minor event in the long and complicated history of the quarrels among the Spaniards.

Even before the expedition left Panama, Pizarro's negotiations in Spain had laid the groundwork for jealousy and resentment, particularly in Almagro. When Hernando Pizarro returned from Spain in 1534 with new grants of land for his brother and for Almagro, the latter discovered that his grants lay far to the south and in very difficult country. An expedition to inspect his new land convinced Almagro that he had been cheated; he seized Cuzco and in so doing opened a civil war that kept the colony in turmoil. Almagro was executed, his son and supporters were stripped of their lands. The Almagro faction, reacting to the attacks of the Pizarro camp, invaded Francisco Pizarro's home and assassinated him.

The presence of Vaca de Castro, an official sent by Charles V to restore order in Peru, was of little help. He first refused to deal with the younger Almagro who was captured in battle and executed. The death of Almagro in effect marked the end of the feuding between the two factions, but new troubles soon arose. Shortly after the arrival of Vaca de Castro, the promulgation of the New Laws posed serious problems for the landholders, whose wealth consisted of *encomiendas*, grants of land together with the inhabiting Indians. The New Laws, intended to prevent oppression of the Indians, provided that exceptionally large *encomiendas* were to be reduced in size and that no *encomienda* was to be hereditary; a failure to fulfill certain duties relating to the Indians would mean loss of an *encomienda*. All those who had taken part in the quarrels between Pizarro and Almagro were faced with the loss of their newly acquired lands. Gonzalo Pizarro found himself the leader of a revolt against the king's representatives who were charged with the government of the colony and thus with the enforcement of the highly unpopular New Laws. Blasco Núñez Vela, appointed first viceroy after the utter failure of Vaca de Castro to cope with the difficult situation, was deposed locally. Gonzalo Pizarro was proclaimed governor and thus became a rebel against royal authority. A priest, Pedro de Gasca, was next sent by Charles and his ministers as president of the *audiencia*, charged with the duty of restoring order to the troubled colony and of bringing the insubordinate conquerors to terms. De Gasca's skill and tact gave him the victory. After his defeat in 1548, Gonzalo Pizarro was executed. Royal authority, bringing with it comparative peace and order, was established in Peru for the first time since the arrival of the Spaniards sixteen years earlier.

Against this background of turmoil, the Inca Garcilaso spent his early years in the former Incan capital of Cuzco. Born almost exactly a year after the execution of the elder Almagro, he was nine years old when Gonzalo Pizarro met his final defeat and the worst of the civil strife was ended. Although Cuzco had been replaced by the new City of the Kings, or Lima as it came to be called, as the center of Spanish activity, the old capital still retained some of its former glory and importance; many of the conquerors settled there because it was convenient to their estates. Perhaps because it was not the seat of government, Cuzco was the place where plots and counterplots were hatched. It became a kind of crossroads. Sooner or later nearly every Spaniard of any consequence passed through it; many of them were entertained by Captain Garcilaso de la Vega. Armies of all factions were seen from time to time in the town, sometimes merely passing through, other times bent upon the destruction of their enemies resident in Cuzco. All of this left its mark upon the young mestizo. Writing many years later, he remarks in a letter to one of his Spanish admirers, "In my childhood I studied a little grammar, badly taught by seven teachers that we had at various times, and worse learned by us students who were but few more in number, because of the upheaval of the wars that were taking place in the country which contributed to the uneasiness of the teachers." [3] It is not surprising that Garcilaso should have kept a vivid memory of his early years since his father was one of Gonzalo Pizarro's most ardent supporters and was intimately involved in the rebellion against the New Laws.

In the early days of the conquest, the lusty Spanish soldiers, deprived of the company of their own women, sought solace in the arms of the Indian women. Men of rank generally did not marry their Indian mistresses, but set up households based upon an informal arrangement which was socially acceptable and which was not frowned upon by the Church. Captain Garcilaso de la Vega provided well enough for his Indian princess at least so far as domestic comforts were concerned, and during the time they lived together apparently showed her affection and consideration. The family occupied an imposing house on the west side of Cuzco, not one of the original Indian structures but one built for one Pedro de Oñate, purchased by Garcilaso after its first owner was killed in battle. It seems doubtful that his son was born there; rather this household was established when the boy was three or four years old. In any case, it is only this house that he mentions when he reminisces about his childhood.

Captain Garcilaso was evidently a gregarious sort for the house seems to have been constantly filled with guests. He did not confine his hospitality to his countrymen but allowed his concubine to entertain numbers of her noble relatives; one has the impression, reading the accounts of the Inca, that he could always find about the house an Indian relative to regale him with stories of the last great days of the empire, the legends handed down from generation to generation.

It is most probable that Garcilaso's first language was Quechua rather than Spanish. His mother, even at the time of her death, spoke little or no Spanish; her will, dated November 22, 1571, was made through an interpreter and was signed by one of the witnesses because the testatrix "said that she did not know how to sign her name." Garcilaso himself, in his prologue to his translation of León Hebreo's *Dialoghi d'amore*, makes a special point of the fact that his native language was neither Italian, in which the dialogues were written, nor Spanish, the language of his translation, but rather the Indian tongue of his mother's people. It is to be doubted, however, that much time passed before he began to use Spanish. Probably neither Quechua nor Spanish was a foreign tongue to him but both were learned during his very early years. His statement about his native language is perhaps not to be taken too literally; after he left Peru and took up residence in Spain, he was always at great pains to identify himself, proudly, as an Indian and furthermore as an Indian of royal blood. Referring to Spanish as a foreign language would support his role as Indian.

Despite his pride in his Indian blood and despite the fact that he frequently speaks of his mother with considerable affection, he is extraordinarily reticent in giving information about her and her family. He tells us that her Indian name was Chimpu Ocllo, that she was baptized and received the name Isabel, that she was the daughter of Huallpa Tupac. That in essence is the extent of his revelations about her. In view of Garcilaso's insistence upon his own identification as an Indian, and in view of the many and detailed references to his father's career and family, one may wonder at the strange unwillingness to discuss his mother. A number of possibilities suggest themselves; the least attractive is that he may have felt some embarrassment about her status as his father's mistress. It is not

[21]

impossible that he truly had little to tell about her, that she became for him, as she is for modern readers, a shadowy figure in the background. About 1551, when Garcilaso's father married Luisa Martel de los Ríos, the Indian princess departed and later married one Juan de Pedroche, a Spanish merchant of Cuzco. Garcilaso remained with his father and stepmother. There is no indication of what his relations with his mother were after the break, though he seems to have continued to visit her and her relatives.

Little enough is known of Garcilaso's childhood and adolescence in Cuzco; the only information available is what he himself casually inserts in his works, principally in the *Comentarios reales* and the *Historia general del Perú*. For a man whose later reputation was to depend entirely upon his intellectual achievements, Garcilaso's early education was singularly sketchy. While it was by no means unusual, even in the sixteenth century, for sons of the rich and noble families in Spain to receive an adequate education, at least on the elementary level, conditions in Peru were scarcely ideal for regular, uninterrupted instruction. Reference has already been made to the disquieting effect of the constant warfare on the teachers and pupils, which undoubtedly made concentration in the classroom difficult when far more exciting events were taking place outside. His first lessons were given by a tutor, Juan de Alcobaza, a friend of the family. After Alcobaza came a series of teachers, none of whom endured long in the post. The last stage of his formal education in Cuzco was with Juan de Cuéllar, canon of the cathedral of Cuzco, who established a school for the sons of the prominent citizens of the city. Here Garcilaso studied Latin along with a group of his contemporaries, some of them mestizos, some Indians and some Spaniards. Garcilaso himself is a little vague as to how long he remained with Cuéllar. In the letter previously cited he writes that he was thirteen or fourteen when he had his last lessons; he obviously received enough instruction to enable him to pursue during his first years in Spain a career that demanded something more than the mere ability to read and write. Cuéllar was evidently a man who took his work seriously and who felt that his colonial pupils were capable of far more than could be offered them in Peru. He is reported to have remarked to them, "Oh, my sons, how I should like to see a dozen of you in the University of Salamanca."

Garcilaso's education was not confined to the classroom; it was during the period of his schooling that Peru was kept in a state of upheaval by the quarrelling factions within the colony. Often enough the turbulence became something more than a conversation among his elders overheard by the boy; violence became a direct part of his experience. Looking back over several decades to the earlier days of his childhood, he often adds a personal note to his account of events which, even as he wrote, were beginning to recede into the shadowy limbo of man's past deeds.

When Gonzalo Pizarro in 1544 undertook the leadership of the Spanish landholders in their protest against the provisions of the New Laws, Captain Garcilaso de la Vega joined him in the belief that Pizarro was mounting a campaign against rebel Indians. It was not long, however, before it became clear that Pizarro and his supporters were in fact in open rebellion against the authority of the King. With that realization, Captain Garcilaso and a number of his friends withdrew from the campaign and returned to Cuzco on their way to Lima to place themselves at the service of the Viceroy Núñez Vela. Pizarro quickly recovered from the loss of so many valuable partisans and with new strength gained from reinforcements who joined him, turned upon Cuzco; there he had his vengeance of Captain Garcilaso and gave the captain's son his first experience of personal danger.

His first act was to draw off the Indians from the captain's estates and to sack the buildings. He was on the point of setting fire to the Indians' houses but was dissuaded by one of his men. In the main house, eight people, the Inca Garcilaso, his mother and sister, Juan de Alcobaza, his son and his brother, along with two Indian servants, were trapped. According to the Inca, they would all have perished at the hands of Pizarro had it not been for the influence of some of his men who remained well disposed toward the captain despite his defection. Even though the inhabitants were spared, the house remained under siege. All the Indians on the estate were forbidden under penalty of death to enter the house, but the loyalty of some to the captain and his family was so great that they risked their lives to bring in at night baskets of corn to feed the captives. One of the neighbors offered to give the young Garcilaso dinner and supper; it was necessary to refuse the evening meal because it was too dangerous to open the door of the house after dark "for we were afraid that at any moment they would murder us." The siege lasted eight months with the house under bombardment from a neighboring house belonging to one of Pizarro's rebels. Even allowing for the fact that many of the details he gives to the unhappy time were in all likelihood supplied to him later, the experience of those eight months must have had a lasting effect upon the five-year-old boy.

Although Captain Garcilaso seems to have had extreme difficulty in guessing who would be the winner in the long, drawn-out struggle between royal authority and Gonzalo Pizarro, he did have extraordinary good fortune in emerging with his life, a good fortune not shared by all his companions. After the events of 1544, it must have been clear that Pizarro was going to be the victor. Captain Garcilaso made his peace with Pizarro and thus was with him at the great battle of Huarina in 1547. Gonzalo Pizarro was the man of the hour and was given what resembled a Roman triumph when he entered Cuzco. The Inca Garcilaso was an eyewitness of the joyful entry; the preceding day he had gone out to meet his father in a village three leagues from Cuzco. His trip to the military camp was made on foot in the company of two Indians who took turns carrying him when he became tired. The return to Cuzco was glorious, however, for the boy was given a horse to ride.

The pageant was carefully arranged to impress both Indians and Spaniards. The Indians were encouraged to celebrate the great event as they had been accustomed to celebrate the arrival of their emperors. They built triumphal arches decorated with the flowers they had traditionally used, they lined the streets, on the orders of the Spanish stage manager, shouting the epithets formerly applied to their own rulers. With magnificent display, the infantry entered first, followed by the cavalry. Then, after a dramatic delay, Gonzalo Pizarro, accompanied only by his servants, as though to divorce himself from the military aspects of the occasion, appeared and made his way to the sound of trumpets and the shouts of the crowds to a church where he paused to pray before retiring to the house of one of his lieutenants.

The scene was impressive. Many years later, writing his history of Peru, the Inca Garcilaso remarks, "I saw everything I have related and could also tell in which house each and every captain was lodged, for I knew them all and I remember the houses even though the events we are describing occurred nearly sixty years ago, because the memory keeps better what was seen in childhood than what occurs in later years."

Throughout his life Garcilaso retained a prejudice in favor of Gonzalo Pizarro, not so much, perhaps, because he was a rebel against authority—that was totally foreign to Garcilaso's nature— but because of Captain Garcilaso's long association with Pizarro and probably even more because of the Inca Garcilaso's own close contact with the ill-fated conqueror. Pizarro had spent the winter after his victory at Huarina in Cuzco; it was probably during this time that Garcilaso formed his favorable opinion. He tells us that he visited Pizarro's house nearly every day, attracted undoubtedly by the companionship of Pizarro's son Fernando and his nephew Francisco, son of the first conqueror. Garcilaso observed Pizarro's manner toward the people with whom he had dealings, from his chief lieutenant to the passerby on the street. Garcilaso was impressed by the great man's unfailing courtesy: he raised his hat to everyone, used the properly formal manner of address to all who—because of their rank—deserved it, displayed proper humility in never allowing his hand to be kissed. All this earned for him honor and respect from his soldiers and from the citizens of Cuzco.

On at least two occasions, the Inca Garcilaso was singularly honored, invited to eat at the great man's table. Pizarro always dined in public at the head of a long table which seated, at the least, a hundred of his soldiers. Two places were left vacant on either side of the leader's chair and in one of these he placed Garcilaso and gave him food from his own plate. Such flattering attention gave Pizarro a great admirer and, much later, a defender. Garcilaso maintained that Pizarro was much maligned by the accusations of historians who must, he asserts, have received false impressions from informers motivated by hatred and rancor.

The comparatively peaceful interlude of the winter of 1547–1548 was the last for Pizarro. To restore order, the priest, Pedro de la Gasca, had been sent from Spain as president of the *audiencia* of Peru, the high court of the colony possessing military, political and judicial authority. He successfully put an end to the Pizarro rebellion at the battle of Sacsahuaman in 1548. With another timely shift of allegiance, Captain Garcilaso de la Vega once more found himself allied with the victor. The Inca Garcilaso was thus given the opportunity to meet another of the leading figures of the time when la Gasca paid a visit to his father's home shortly after Pizarro and the other leaders of the rebellion were executed in Cuzco. The Inca Garcilaso apparently did not witness the executions but he did see the severed heads of some of the rebels displayed in iron cages in the square of Cuzco as a deterrent to further disloyal activities. Francisco de Carvajal, Pizarro's right-hand man, was hanged, drawn and quartered and parts of the body were left on each of the four main roads leading out of Cuzco. Garcilaso relates a particularly gruesome episode in which he and some of his young friends, all under twelve years of age, went to the outskirts of town to see the decaying body.

Garcilaso's role in most of the stirring events of his youth was that of observer or, at best, that of passive participant. In one episode, however, he did acquit himself nobly as the juvenile hero. Between the death of the second viceroy Antonio de Mendoza in 1553 and the arrival of his successor Andrés Hurtado de Mendoza in 1555, the colony was governed by the judges of the *audiencia;* it was in this interval that the last significant phase of the civil wars disturbed the peace. Francisco Hernández Girón led a powerful insurrection against the government in protest once more against the New Laws and to establish the right of the Spanish landholders to forced labor from the Indians.

Girón chose to give his campaign a dramatic beginning. The occasion for the attack was to be a fashionable wedding in Cuzco on November 13, 1553. The wedding was properly celebrated with games and feasts. That afternoon, to watch the games in progress in the street, the Inca Garcilaso climbed onto a stone wall facing the house where Girón was staying. He saw Girón sitting at a window, "his arms crossed on his breast, his head down, more pensive and withdrawn than melancholy itself. He must have been thinking about what he was to do that night." (*Historia General de Perú,* Book VII, Ch. 2) The wedding feast was an elegant affair with all the town's prominent citizens in attendance. Garcilaso arrived at the end of the banquet to accompany his father and stepmother home. The corregidor, seeing that there were no vacant places at the table, had just invited Garcilaso to stand beside his chair when the feast was interrupted by loud knocks on the door announcing the arrival of Girón who entered with drawn sword.

In the ensuing confusion, all the candles but one were extinguished and two guests were slain immediately. The corregidor had prudently removed himself as soon as he saw that Girón was no welcome addition to the festivities. Since none of the guests was armed, they quickly followed. Garcilaso, with his father and some thirty-six others, escaped from the house via the roof. By means of a ladder they had found, they reached the street. Garcilaso was pressed into service as a scout. At each intersection he advanced and, as soon as he saw that the way was clear, whistled as a sign for his elders to proceed. They made their way to the house belonging to Captain Garcilaso's brother-in-law where they laid plans to go to Lima to offer their services to the *audiencia.* The young Garcilaso was sent home for his father's horse. The men made their escape, leaving Garcilaso to make his way home again, there anxiously to await further events.

Garcilaso's childhood was filled with war and bloodshed, but there were times when he had the chance to learn something besides violence in the world around him. He played games in the mighty fortress of Sacsahuaman, located just north of Cuzco, and, whether or not as a child he was conscious that his playground was the scene of one of the world's most impressive engineering feats, he was aware of the complexities of the structure and of the danger of becoming lost in its labyrinthine passages. He and his friends dared not go beyond the point where the sunlight ended, so impressed were they by the frightening tales told by the Indians of the dangers within. In this fortress Garcilaso saw the evidence of Spanish disregard for Indian monuments; as soon as they began to build houses they started to carry off stones from the fortress and left it in ruins.

He was well acquainted with other parts of the city, too, with its reminders of the glorious empire now destroyed and the new structures arising everywhere to meet the needs of Europeans. He observed the Indians gradually losing their traditions and the knowledge of earlier generations. In the Temple of the Sun there had been five fountains when the temple was the religious center of the empire. Finally only one was left functioning to irrigate the garden of the monastery which replaced the pagan temple. Through lack of maintenance this last fountain eventually ceased to operate; the Indians could not repair it because there was not one left in the city who knew the source of the water.

Indian traditions were not completely lost in the years immediately following the Spanish conquest; many of them survive even today. Garcilaso, though he lived in a Spanish household after his father's marriage, was educated in the Spanish tradition and was in constant contact with the influential white masters of the Indians, was never far removed from Indian life. While he lived with his mother he learned from her and from her friends and relatives the Indian ways and absorbed the Indian spirit. Nearly every week the princess received visits from the few members of the royal family who had escaped Atahualpa's massacre; in Chapter 15, Book I of his *Comentarios reales,* Garcilaso relates that during these visits "their usual conversations were about the origin of their kings, about their majesty, about the greatness of their empire, about their conquests and exploits, about the government they had in peace and in war, about the laws which they ordained for the well-being of their vassals."

Garcilaso learned the use of *quipu,* the Inca method of keeping records with series of knotted strings. He became so expert that when the Indians came to pay their tributes twice a year, it was Garcilaso to whom they turned to have the accounts checked. They did not trust the Spaniards and were satisfied they were not being cheated only when Garcilaso assured them that the written Spanish account agreed with their *quipu* records. He became familiar with the music of the Indians, the reed flutes they played, and the folk songs that celebrated the Inca wars and heroic deeds. He acquired some familiarity with the Indian poetry and the themes it celebrated. He had a demonstration of the Indian knowledge of geography in the scale model of Cuzco built of clay, sticks and small stones to give a realistic idea of the physical characteristics of the city. It was the custom for each group within the empire to make such models of the towns and provinces within the area. Lacking any other means of recording geographical knowledge, they used these models as moderns do maps. Garcilaso also apparently knew something of the Indian methods in geometry, though he modestly refrains from elaborating on it. He had experience of Indian medicine, both theoretical and practical, sometimes as patient and at least once as practitioner. By applying a certain herb, Garcilaso restored the use of an eye that had all but fallen out of its socket. Later in Spain he met his erstwhile patient who swore that the diseased eye was now stronger than the other.

The imposition of Spanish rule upon the Indians and the introduction of Christian festivals did not entirely annihilate the native celebrations, though the feasts that Garcilaso witnessed were but a pale reflection of the magnificent events held in the old days, at least according to his Indian informants. The festival of Collcampata, so called from the name of the area in front of the great fortress of Cuzco, was devoted to the ritual plowing of the field dedicated to the sun. Only members of the royal family were allowed to till this soil which they did each year according to an established formula. The work was done rhythmically with the accompaniment of songs whose verses punned on the word *haylli,* triumph, the men turning the soil with spade-like instruments, the women removing the weeds. Garcilaso witnessed the ceremony as performed by the Indians and also an adaptation of it made by the choir master of the cathedral who saw an opportunity to turn a pagan festival to

Christian use. For the feast of the Holy Sacrament, eight of Garcilaso's young mestizo friends, dressed as Indians and each with a plow in his hand, formed a procession accompanied by a choir singing words composed especially for the occasion. The Indians were delighted that one of their old rituals should serve their new religion.

Another festival, witnessed at least in part by Garcilaso, was intended to clear the city of disease and other evils. At dawn, four Indians of royal blood, armed with lances, ran through the four main streets of the city driving before them evil spirits. At night, the ceremony was repeated to rid the city of nocturnal evils, but with flaming torches instead of lances. The burned-out torches were thrown into the stream to be carried away to the sea. Garcilaso never saw the nighttime performance because it took place after his bedtime. He explains that the custom survived in his time, not to drive out evil spirits, since the Indians were becoming enlightened, but in memory of past ages because there were still some old Indians who had not been baptized. If their elders were enlightened, the Indian children were not; Garcilaso recalls they fled in terror from one of the torches, infested with evil spirits, that had been left in the street. Garcilaso confesses that at the time he did not know why the thing was so strenuously avoided, and that if he had known he too would have fled.

In the periods of quiet between military upheavals, Garcilaso saw something more of Peru than Cuzco and its immediate environs. He accompanied his father on inspection tours of his estates and observed the life of the rural Indians. He travelled over much of Upper Peru, a good distance to the south of Cuzco, and it is generally assumed, on the basis of a poetic but factual description of the great silver mines, that he spent some time at Potosí.

Along with the gradual decay of Indian ways, he witnessed the complementary increase of European influence on the society and economy of Peru. He observed in the countryside the introduction of European weapons. He confesses, in his account of Hernando de Soto's expedition to Florida, that he and his friends suffered from the lack of opportunity to study their letters and from an excess of opportunity to study the art of war. He laments that in this he was most unfortunate; if he had had more training in letters and less in arms he would not have found it so difficult to express his thoughts. Be that as it may, he kept alive his interest in horses and in Spain acquired a certain fame as a breeder.

Whatever the deprivations Garcilaso suffered in Peru, his problems were not financial ones. His father, the captain, had displayed great skill in avoiding the many dangers presented by the disturbed conditions in the colony. His wealth and influence increased constantly and in 1554, he was named Corregidor, or Chief Magistrate, of Cuzco, an office he held until the new viceroy, Andrés Hurtado de Mendoza, replaced him. His former association with rebels may have given rise to a certain mistrust of the captain's loyalty. He did not long survive and, after a long illness, died in 1559.

After his father's death Garcilaso decided, for reasons that are not entirely clear, to go to Spain. It seems fairly certain that Garcilaso was no longer in a favorable financial position even though he had been given, some time earlier, one of his father's estates. In his will, Captain Garcilaso left the bulk of his wealth to his widow and two daughters and provided four thousand pesos for his natural son to study in Spain. It may be that the decision to go to Spain was motivated primarily by his father's bequest but it also became obvious later that the young mestizo had somehow seized upon the idea that the captain's services to the Crown had not been properly rewarded and that an appeal to a generous monarch would result in an easing of the financial strain. For whatever reason or combination of reasons—he may have felt that his future in Peru was in doubt—he made arrangements to leave Cuzco in 1560.

The courtesy call that Garcilaso paid to the Corregidor of Cuzco on the eve of his departure became a memorable occasion. The Corregidor took him into a room where he showed him the mummies of five of his royal ancestors, the Inca Viracocha, Tupac Inca Yupanqui, Huayna Capac and two queens, Mama Runtu and Mama Ocllo. As he left his native land, Garcilaso was forcibly reminded of his imperial blood and saw, as the mummies were carried through the streets, how the Indians knelt and wept and the Spaniards removed their caps.

The experiences of Garcilaso's first twenty years in Peru were in many ways the most significant of his life. By far the greater part of his life was spent in Spain where, except for brief, casual meetings with other natives of Peru, he had no direct contact with his own people. Perhaps because of a feeling of inferiority arising from his mixed blood, he apparently tried to slough off his Indian heritage in his early years in Spain in order to identify himself with Spain and to make a European career for himself, a career in which a colonial and Indian background was of no particular advantage. Whatever successes or failures he may have experienced in Spain, in the end he turned back to his youth and found in it the source of his greatest success, the material for his *Comentarios reales*. It was not only the basic inspiration for the work, a wish to see the Incan civilization given its due place in history, but even more the subjective, emotional element in it that derived from his life in that strange world of sixteenth-century Peru where society was neither Indian nor Spanish, but a mixture of the two. All the things he saw, heard and did there remained a part of him and were translated to the pages of his history of Peru. Nearly half a century may have dulled some of the sharpness of his memories, but it never erased them.

III   *The Years in Montilla*

Garcilaso's life in Cuzco is comparatively easy to trace in its broad outlines since in all his writings he was accustomed to insert bits of information about his activities and experiences.[4] The picture changes, however, after he left Peru and he remains for the most part silent about the life he found in Spain. This has given rise to a great deal of speculation, much of it sentimental and romantic, about what really happened to him. The attitudes displayed by Garcilaso in his works, written when he was no longer a young man, were often querulous and his insistence upon being thought of as an Indian, his apparent desire to reject his Spanish blood gave the impression of a defensive frame of mind; his frequent complaints about his poverty led his readers to the conclusion that his life must indeed have been miserable. It was known that he lived in Montilla in the province of Córdoba, and it was assumed that he was forced to drag out his days in the stifling atmosphere of a small town which did not benefit even from the backwash of Spain's great period of artistic and literary activity. It was presumed by some that he must have encountered so much prejudice because of his mixed blood that his situation was all but intolerable. Lacking any definite statements from Garcilaso himself, it is probably impossible now to know whether there were unpleasant incidents, but there are very strong indications that Garcilaso was accepted by Montilla and its citizens and that existence there, while perhaps not precisely exciting, was far from intolerable to him.

In the past thirty years, devoted and painstaking searches of notarial and ecclesiastical records, by Spanish and Peruvian scholars especially, have produced enough evidence to trace the Inca's career in Spain more accurately. To be sure, the dry and formal records cannot reveal the man's inner life, but they may offer hints. Despite all the documents now available, there are periods in Garcilaso's life when one could wish for more information.

The trip from Cuzco was a long one, by land to Lima, by sea to Panama, overland again across the isthmus to take ship across the Atlantic to Lisbon. From Lisbon he sailed to Seville, a city that delighted him with its charms. After a short stay there he apparently went to his father's native province, Extremadura, for his first meeting with his Spanish relatives. His next stop was Montilla where his father's brother, Alonso de Vargas, was then living.

When Garcilaso arrived in 1561, his uncle had been established there for some six years, having been retired with pension from the service of Charles V, in which "he spent in the three parts of the Old World thirty-eight years of his life fighting against Moors, Turks and heretics and against the enemies of the Crown of Spain." [5] After settling in Montilla he had married Doña Luisa Ponce de León, the daughter of a local family with good connections. Her brother, Francisco de Argote, was the father of the poet Luis de Góngora y Argote.

The town of Montilla was a part of the feudal estate of the Marquises de Priego, whose family was related to that of Alonso de Vargas, and consequently of Garcilaso, and his wife. The affairs of the town during Garcilaso's residence there were efficiently managed first by two women who held the title and less efficiently perhaps by their two male successors. Garcilaso seems to have been on good terms with the two women; in speaking of the connections between the two families, he refers to the marquises as his natural lords and expresses his desire to serve as loyal vassal. His particular praise is for the two marchionesses whom he extols for their magnanimity and Christian virtue; the men of the family are not mentioned by name, a silence that may be taken to indicate something less than a warm relationship with them, due perhaps to their lack of promptness in meeting their financial obligations to Garcilaso.

Montilla was not without claims to fame. It was the birthplace of the Great Captain, Gonzalo Fernández de Córdoba, whose name has become legendary in Spain. It was the Great Captain who, after good service in the wars against the Moors and in the campaign against Granada, successfully drove the French out of Sicily and Naples and so restored those kingdoms to Ferdinand of Aragon. The independent spirit of the captain's nephew who refused to give up his house in Córdoba for the use of one of the king's officers and instead held him prisoner in his castle all but brought disaster upon the family. Ferdinand's anger was assuaged somewhat by the Great Captain's intervention, but still he ordered the castle in Montilla levelled. Montilla acquired a certain renown thanks to one of Miguel de Cervantes' *Exemplary Novels*, "The Colloquy of the Dogs," in which he refers to a well-known witch of the town. La Camacha, as she was called, was supposed to have exercised her talents on a member of the Priego family and to have turned him into a horse. Cervantes apparently heard the stories about her during a brief stay in the town in 1591. If current identification as Elvira García la Camacha is correct, she must have been known to Garcilaso for she was a prosperous merchant of the town; her will was witnessed in 1569 by the priest Francisco de Castro, a friend of Garcilaso and his proxy in some of his business affairs.

While Alonso de Vargas enjoyed the rank of *hidalgo,* or gentleman, and undoubtedly had social privileges because of his double connection with the local feudal lords, his nephew's place in the town's social hierarchy was less well defined. Garcilaso had no letters patent to qualify him as a *hidalgo;* he lacked the income necessary to be enrolled as a *caballero contioso,* that is, one who, because he was rich enough to outfit himself, was obliged to serve the king in time of war and who had the privilege of serving on the town council. He evidently could not be enrolled as a citizen because of his blood relationship with the Priego family. All this left him with the status of visitor dependent upon the generous acceptance of his uncle and the ruling family. Such a situation must have seemed an uncomfortable one to the mestizo who had enjoyed a privileged position in Cuzco.

When it was that Garcilaso made his decision to remain in Montilla it is impossible to know, but he was warmly welcomed from the beginning by the retired captain who become so attached to Garcilaso that he treated him as if he were his own son. Shortly after his arrival in Montilla, Garcilaso's financial status was improved; on September 16, 1561, Don Alonso appeared before a notary to declare that Gómez Suárez de Figueroa was the legitimate and only heir of Leonor de Vargas, his paternal aunt.

Sometime after November 24, 1561, when he acted as godfather in Montilla, Garcilaso went to Madrid to press his claims for reward and favor from the King. His contention was that his father's services n the conquest of Peru had not been properly rewarded, that on 's father's death his children (apparently the illegitimate offspring of Isabel) were left unprovided for, and that his mother's patrimony should be restored. Garcilaso is not entirely clear as to what he means by this last. He pressed his case before the Council of the Indies, the supreme policy-making body for Spain's colonies in the New World, where he felt everything was going well. He thought that he had convinced the members of the Council that his claims had merit when Lope García de Castro raised the question that was to kill all hope of success.

García de Castro, who was later sent to Peru as governor, had read accounts of the civil wars in the colony damaging to the elder Garcilaso. Francisco López de Gómara's *Historia general de las Indias,* Diego de Fernández' *Crónica del Perú* and Agustín de Zárate's *Historia del descubrimiento y conquista del Perú,* all reported that during the battle of Huarina Gonzalo Pizarro found himself in great danger because his horse was lost; his life was saved, and consequently the rebellion continued, only because Captain Garcilaso gave Pizarro his own horse. For García de Castro this was evidence enough that the captain's services were not all in the best interests of the King and that he should really have been treated as a rebel. Garcilaso's arguments that the historians had given a false account of events were of no avail; his assertion that Pizarro took the horse only after the battle was finished and that therefore his father's action could have had no influence on the outcome of the battle merely provoked the scorn of the Council.

Disappointed by the failure of his efforts in Madrid, Garcilaso went to Seville with the idea of returning to Peru, evidently having forgotten the provision in his father's will for his education in Spain. On June 27, 1563, he applied for the necessary permission to make the trip which was never realized, either because the application was refused or because Garcilaso had second thoughts on the matter. How long he stayed in Seville and how he passed his time there is still unknown. He made arrangements to have his father's remains brought from Peru and buried in the church of San Isidro in Seville, though it seems doubtful that the reburial, given the inevitable delays in securing permission and the difficulties of transportation, could have been accomplished during his stay in Seville in 1563, for he was back in Montilla on November 17, 1563, where he remained at least until the end of the year. It is more likely that reburial took place in 1579 when Garcilaso was again in S though for what reason he does not say.

Until he returned to Montilla after his frustrating expe

Madrid and Seville, Garcilaso was known both in Peru and in Spain as Gómez Suárez de Figueroa. The last time he is known to have used that name is in a baptismal record of November 17, 1563; on November 22 of that same year he is identified as Garcilaso de la Vega. Occasionally in later documents the more familiar Garcilaso de la Vega is accompanied by a statement to the effect that he was formerly known as Gómez Suárez de Figueroa. He did not add the royal title of Inca until later and only in the last few years of his life is the title found consistently as a part of his name. The adoption of his father's name was very probably due to practical reasons and no doubt indicates a decision to stay in Montilla. The name of the second son of the Priego family was also Gómez Suárez de Figueroa. Besides the confusion likely to be caused by the presence in the small town of two men of exactly the same name, it may well be that Garcilaso's family felt it more tactful for the young mestizo, whose standing in the community was at that time not of the most solid, to adopt another name. Alonso de Vargas had, after all, established a precedent in the family; he had been known as Francisco de Plasencia during his campaign in Flanders.

The records of Montilla contain no reference to Garcilaso for the year 1564. It has generally been assumed that at this time he enlisted in the army and served in Italy. There is at present no documentary evidence for such a stage in his career. If he did begin his military career at this time, it was limited almost exactly to a year since he is recorded as having acted as godfather in Montilla on December 30, 1563, and again on January 1, 1565.

Garcilaso remained in Montilla almost constantly for the next four or five years, though he undoubtedly made short visits to other towns in the area. He continued to live with his uncle and doña Luisa; stables were added to the house for the specific use of Garcilaso so he was able to indulge his interest in horses. His success with his animals is attested by the town council's choice in 1579 of one of his horses as an approved sire. Garcilaso must have earned the respect and affection of a number of the townspeople for his name appears with great frequency in parish records as godfather to the children of the town. He seems to have had few business affairs at this time, reasonably enough since his wealth was limited to his inheritances from his father and his aunt. The only transaction recorded is his purchase of a mulatto slave for sixty ducats.

One can only speculate on how Garcilaso filled his days; most likely he shared in whatever social life his uncle's family enjoyed and in the local religious and civil ceremonies. He was apparently on friendly terms with the local clergy. In many places he speaks approvingly of the Jesuits both in Peru and in Spain; since the order operated a school in Montilla it is probable that Garcilaso was in close touch with them. Although he is silent upon the matter, at some time he must have begun during those quiet years to extend the sketchy education he reports he had in Peru. Certainly at some time he had to acquire the knowledge and skills necessary for a literary career. If he did not make a trip to Italy, he may well have devoted himself to the study of Italian at this time.

For two periods, August, 1568 to March, 1569, and June, 1569 to March, 1570, no documents have been found in the Montilla archives relating to Garcilaso. Assuming that he would have continued his usual activities as popular godfather, and assuming that the archival records are complete (perhaps too great an assumption), Garcilaso must have been absent from Montilla during those times. It has generally been assumed that he began his military career then. The rebellion of the Moors in the province of Granada had broken out in December of 1567 and continued to plague Philip II until it was finally quelled in 1570. Whether or not Garcilaso did serve in the campaign against the Moors as early as 1568–1569 is in doubt. The first indication of his military activity is his commission as captain signed by the King on March 4, 1570.[6] On March 17, 1570, Garcilaso appeared before a notary to appoint Francisco de Castro as his substitute in the office of executor of his uncle's will. The reason given is that Garcilaso was in the service of the King and of the marquis, his natural lord, in the war of Granada. Two other commissions as captain, that is to say, permission to recruit a company of soldiers, are on record dated June 27, 1570, signed by Don Juan de Austria and August 30, 1570, signed by the King.

The military duties required of Garcilaso must have allowed him a great deal of freedom for he was able to return to Montilla fairly frequently. The scene of the war was not far from Montilla and, granted a certain lack of rigidity in the military structure, he may well have been able to make quick trips to Montilla to take care of affairs connected with settling his uncle's estate. In any case, he was in the town on March 20, July 19, and August 25. He does not reappear until February, 1571.

Garcilaso's military career, whenever it began, was a comparatively short one and in all probability not a particularly successful one. Military life was clearly not entirely to his liking. After his return to Montilla in 1571, there is no further indication of any connection with the army though he continued to use the title of captain until 1579, after which date he is known simply as "señor Garcilaso de la Vega." Perhaps he saw in the army an opportunity to escape from the boredom of Montilla, perhaps he saw himself as carrying on a family tradition. It is also possible that, dreaming of heroic deeds that would attract the favorable attention of Philip and Don Juan de Austria, he looked upon service to the King as a means to gain the rewards that had been denied him earlier. If so, he was again disappointed. A cryptic statement in one of his two surviving letters written in 1592 indicates that his hopes were once more dashed. Speaking of his fondness for arms and horses when he was a boy in Cuzco, he says that he continued such exercises after he came to Spain "until the ingratitude of a certain prince and no reward from the King closed me up in my corner."

The death of his uncle was eventually to make considerable change in Garcilaso's life. The income from the estate was left to doña Luisa for her lifetime, but on her death the property was to be divided between Garcilaso and his aunt, Isabel de Vargas. Garcilaso, after his return from the wars, settled in Montilla again, presumably in the house that was eventually to become his. Legal documents indicate that all was not peace and harmony in the household, perhaps because doña Luisa was dissatisfied with the terms of her husband's will which prevented her from disposing of any of his property.

In 1571 Garcilaso's mother died in Cuzco. Her will, discovered comparatively recently, assumes particular importance in the support it offers for Garcilaso's statements about the Indian princess. Until the will was found, there were no documents to indicate the existence of any such person as Chimpu Ocllo, legitimate offspring of the royal line. One of Garcilaso's severest modern critics, M. Gonzales de la Rosa, maintained that there never was such a person and that this was evidence that Garcilaso lied in everything that he wrote. Her will, in which she is identified by the name adopted after her baptism, Isabel Suárez, states that she was the legitimate daughter of Huallpa Tupac and Cusi Chimbo, that she was the wife of Juan del Pedroche, and that she had two legitimate daughters. She also referred to her son, Gómez Suárez, and made provisions concerning the coca plantation, Havisco, the income from which Garcilaso had assigned to her when he went to Spain. It was not until 1574 that Garcilaso gave power of attorney to three residents of Cuzco for the sale of the plantation.

If the death of his uncle did not immediately benefit Garcilaso financially, it did produce a change in his activities. As executor of the will, Garcilaso was in effect the manager of the estate and so found himself far more involved in business affairs than ever before. There is no indication that he moved from his uncle's house; he probably continued to occupy it with doña Luisa until her removal to Córdoba in 1581. It may have been during the period after his uncle's death that Garcilaso turned his attention more seriously to intellectual matters; he remarks at one point that because he had so much leisure time, a polite way of saying he was bored, he began to translate León Hebreo's *Dialoghi d'amore*. Although the translation was not published until 1590, his dedication to the King is dated January 19, 1586, which would indicate that work on the translation had been begun some considerable time earlier. Garcilaso himself intimates that the task cost him a great deal of time and effort. He began to consider other projects while he was still in Montilla; the composition of the *Florida* was under way by 1586 and he was considering a treatise on the conquest of Peru in which he would elaborate more upon the ancient customs of the Indians than any non-Indian could hope to do.

Little else seems to have affected the course of his life until 1581, when doña Luisa moved to Córdoba, leaving Garcilaso in sole possession of the Montilla house. He did make at least one trip to Seville and one to Badajoz where a branch of the family was established. There are some indications of trips to nearby towns as well, especially to Las Posadas to visit Gonzalo Silvestre on whom he depended heavily for materials incorporated in the *Florida*. His situation changed radically in 1586 when the death of doña Luisa left him absolute master of his half of Don Alonso's estate. From that point on the archival records show a greatly increased activity and indicate that he was a moderately wealthy man.

It is characteristic of Garcilaso to grumble about his poverty.[7] All his published works, most of which were completed after he came into possession of his inheritance, and his surviving letters are filled with complaints about his lack of money. Just how seriously this is to be taken is open to question. Before the death of his aunt, he was certainly not rich; on the other hand, there is no reason to believe that he suffered want. He came to Spain in the hope of reward and favor from the King; he failed in at least one attempt, and possibly more, to gain what he felt was due him. Perhaps he never forgot what might have been and the lack of material recognition haunted him the rest of his life. It has been suggested that all of his complaining comes not from the fact that he was truly poor but that he truly believed himself to be so because he was not able to occupy a position sufficiently exalted for his background. He took great pride in his distinguished ancestry, and was acutely conscious that he was the descendant of royalty, albeit royalty now without a kingdom, and of Spanish heroes, *hidalgos* and nobles. In Montilla he was constantly reminded of his relationship with the local feudal family, yet for many years he could not even claim citizenship in the town. All in all, his life in Montilla was not that of a prince. That he felt he had some claim to noble, if not princely, status is indicated in his assuming the title of Inca to which strictly speaking he had no claim. He recognizes the fact and explains that the emperors of Peru generously allowed certain of their subjects to use the title. One does not read many pages of the *Comentarios reales* without realizing that for Garcilaso the word Inca carried with it the idea of ruler or heir apparent. Obviously, if he considered himself of princely rank, his worldly wealth was never commensurate with it.

Garcilaso is discreet about his private life, but hints of it occasionally appear in unlikely places. In 1930, there was found a copy of some of the treatises of Fray Bartolomé de las Casas, the Dominican Bishop of Chiapa known as the Apostle of the Indies. The book contained two hand-written statements relative to Garcilaso.[8] One owner, Diego de Córdoba, noted that the book was particularly valuable to him because it had belonged to Garcilaso. The second lengthy note was written in 1653 by don Diego's son, Iñigo de Córdoba Ponce de León, who had more interesting information. He identifies the first note as having been written by his father, then adds, "He was an intimate friend of the said Inca Garcilaso de la V. He was truly a man of very good parts and holy life, he was wise and prudent . . . I knew him and remember him very well. He was of average height, dark, very quiet in his speech. He had in Spain a son whom I knew very well and who resembled his father. He died at more than seventy years of age and I judge it was in 1652 . . . He told me many times that he had written [copied?] the *Comentarios reales* which are the books which his father had written about the Indies and that he had written them all by his own hand."

The identity of this son of Garcilaso remained unknown for a number of years. Garcilaso never mentions him or his mother and until 1946 there was no evidence of any kind to support the statement of don Iñigo. In that year documents were found in the archives of the cathedral chapter of Córdoba that not only confirmed the existence of such a son, but identified him and his mother. On March 24, 1620, there is a reference to Diego de Vargas, "natural son of Garcilaso de la Vega, deceased." [9] On March 31 of the same year, Diego de Vargas appeared before the chapter and identified his parents as Garcilaso and Beatriz de Vega. Diego de Vargas was at that time sacristan of the Chapel of the Souls in Purgatory founded by Garcilaso.

Both Diego de Vargas and Beatriz de Vega figure in Garcilaso's will. Each was to receive an annual income of eighty ducats; in the event of his mother's death, Vargas was to receive her income in addition to his own. Beatriz de Vega was also left considerable household equipment. She is identified in the will as a servant in the household; Vargas is referred to as a "citizen of Córdoba whom I have brought up." In both bequests it was stipulated that they would be revoked if either beneficiary should take legal action against the other heirs. How different was Garcilaso's own father's will in which, after specifying the bequest to Garcilaso, he added, ". . . because such is my will because of the love I have for him being as he is my natural son and as such I name and declare him."

Garcilaso's last few years in Montilla were dedicated, in addition to his business affairs, to his literary efforts. The translation of the *Diálogos* was completed and published before he abandoned the town, the *Florida* was well under way, and the *Comentarios reales* were at least planned by 1591, when Garcilaso left Montilla for Córdoba.

IV *Old Age in Córdoba*

The change in scene from Montilla to Córdoba had, on the surface at least, little effect upon the activities of Garcilaso.[10] He continued to act with great frequency as godfather to children of the artisan class especially. Business documents executed before Córdoba notaries are more frequent than in Montilla, though it should be kept in mind that the Montilla archives may not be as complete as those in Córdoba.

His greatest financial problem during the first years of his stay in Córdoba involved the Marqués de Priego. Alonso de Vargas held an encumbrance on the marquis's estate which constituted probably the largest single item of the property he willed to Garcilaso. During the period in which doña Luisa received the income, there seems to have been no particular problem in collecting the payments due. However, the advent of the new marquis, Pedro Fernández de Córdoba y Figueroa, was the source of great annoyance to Garcilaso for the marquis displayed rather a cavalier attitude toward his debts. Between January, 1592, and September, 1602, Garcilaso appointed a series of deputies to collect the money owing him. Their success was varied but they never received more than partial payment. The arrears mounted to such a sum that at the end of 1602 Garcilaso took successful legal action to collect. The marquis, either hard pressed financially himself or simply dilatory, continued to be a bad debtor and each year until his death in 1605 fell behind in his payment. It was not until 1614 that payments on the debt became regular.

Not all Garcilaso's business affairs in his first few years in Córdoba were confined to his dealings with the Marqués de Priego. The legal documents which survive indicate a very active business life, buying and selling real estate, dealing in mortgages and loans, acting as executor for the estate of Gonzalo Silvestre, his chief informant for the *Florida*. Whether because he felt hard pressed for cash or for some other reason, in August, 1605, Garcilaso became *mayordomo* of the Hospital of the Immaculate Conception of Our Lady in Córdoba. His duties there were those of a business manager, responsible for the operation of the hospital. He held the post until mid-1608.

Garcilaso's literary career began in Montilla, but it was in Córdoba that it flowered. Not only the reading, gathering of materials, and writing occupied him; there were many other details of publication that required attention. The translation of the *Diálogos de amor* had been published in Madrid in 1590, before he left Montilla. Evidently it was a successful venture because in 1594 he began to think of a second edition. The royal license, granting Garcilaso permission to publish and exclusive rights, was issued September 7, 1588. On June 1, 1594, he signed all his rights over to Francisco de Garay and Jerónimo Bercedo on the condition that they arrange for republication of the work. Garcilaso was not interested in any monetary rewards from his writing; there is no mention of payment for the rights, and he relinquished all claims to profits from a new edition. Garay and Bercedo did not produce the new edition; on March 1, 1599, six months after the expiration of the royal license, Garcilaso, still hopeful of seeing his work in print again, authorized one Juan de Morales to negotiate an extension of the license for the *Diálogos* and a license for the publication of the *Florida* He also granted Morales power to arrange for publication. Morales was either unsuccessful or uninterested; nothing came of the projects and Garcilaso evidently abandoned plans for a second edition of the *Diálogos*.

More than five years elapsed before Garcilaso made a renewed attempt to obtain a license for the publication of the *Florida*. On December 9, 1604, he authorized Domingo de Silva to secure the necessary permission for the *Florida* and for the *Comentarios reales,* and to make arrangements for the printing and sale of the books once permission was granted. It is noteworthy that Garcilaso provided, in case no better arrangement could be made, that he would pay the costs of a half-printing, that is, 750 copies of each title. Judging from the publication date of the *Florida,* 1605, de Silva was a successful agent. Preliminary plans for publication in Portugal must have been made even before de Silva was authorized to proceed. In November, 1604, approval in advance of the royal license was granted in Lisbon for the *Florida.* In the case of the *Comentarios reales,* there were delays in publication; it finally appeared in Lisbon in 1609. On June 19, 1609, Garcilaso authorized Jerónimo Ferraz, a member of the Company of Jesus in Lisbon, to settle accounts with the printer and to arrange for delivery of the books to the procurator of one of the Company's schools in Seville.

Garcilaso's last work, the *Historia general del Perú,* or second part of the *Comentarios reales,* did not appear until 1617, the year after his death. Arrangements for publication were initiated with an agreement dated October 23, 1614, between Garcilaso and Francisco Romero, bookseller. The agreement is a particularly interesting document for it states in far more detail than any other of Garcilaso's papers the terms under which publication was to be made. The edition was to be of fifteen hundred copies; printing was to be started one month from the date of the agreement and was to be done "in good letter and in good impression." The work was to be completed within ten months. Half the copies were to belong to Romero, half to Garcilaso. Romero was responsible for marketing the books and, whether they were sold for cash, on credit, or traded for other books, he was to settle accounts with Garcilaso a year and one-half after the date of the agreement. So far as expenses of printing were concerned, Garcilaso agreed to pay for the paper used in his 750 copies, payment to be made at the end of each week of the production period. It was further agreed that if Romero had to travel in order to sell the books, Garcilaso would share equally with him the cost of the travel and the cost of transporting the books.

The agreement was not fulfilled for some unknown reason. When the book did appear in 1617, the title page indicated that it was published by the widow of Andrés de Barrera and at her expense. Even though Romero did not carry through as publisher, there was apparently no ill feeling between the two partners; Romero signed as witness to a codicil to Garcilaso's will on April 20, 1616.

His failure in earlier attempts to gain reward and favor from the King continued to rankle in Garcilaso's heart. He felt himself ill-used, the victim of royal parsimony and prejudice. In the "Relación de la descendencia de Garci Pérez de Vargas" he gives vent to his feelings: "One sees everywhere that many who are deserving receive nothing, and others without any merit whatsoever, through the occult favor of the stars rather than through the liberality or prodigality of the prince, receive rewards in abundance." While money is always welcome and Garcilaso felt himself always in need of it, the prospect of financial gain became relatively unimportant to him; proper recognition for his father's and his own services to the Crown became a matter of pride. In 1604 Garcilaso must have had his hopes aroused again by the presence of his nephew, Alonso de Vargas Figueroa, son of Garcilaso's full sister. On June 30, 1604, Garcilaso granted his nephew full power and authority to pursue his claims in Madrid. In plaintive tones he reviews, as he had done before and was to do again, the reasons for which he felt reward was due. The nephew, a resident of Madrid, must have thought that he had some influence in Court circles; it is evident from the document that he had urged Garcilaso to renew his pretensions. It had been the ministers of Philip II who rejected Garcilaso's earlier petitions; the new King, Philip III, might conceivably be more favorably inclined. One of the most interesting features of the document is the fact that Garcilaso relinquishes in favor of Vargas Figueroa all claims to any reward received.

It is unfortunate that legal documents reveal so little of the circumstances that produce them. On July 7, 1611, seven years after the name of Garcilaso's nephew first appears in the archives, Garcilaso once more legally grants him authority to try for royal favor, again with the privilege of keeping for himself any profits from the endeavor. The nephew is now identified as Alonso Márquez Inca de Figueroa. Strangely enough the same agreement was executed before a notary for the third time, November 13, 1614.

That is the last mention of Garcilaso's nephew, but it was not the last of Garcilaso's attempts to collect what he thought was due him. Whether Alonso Márquez Inca de Figueroa died, whether he returned to Cuzco or whether he and his uncle quarrelled, he was replaced as Garcilaso's representative at court. On May 5, 1615, Garcilaso charged Cristóbal de Burgos y Arellano with the same commission and offered the same reward in case of success. Here Garcilaso's statement of his claims is rather more detailed than formerly; in the legal document signed by Garcilaso he makes clear that Burgos y Arellano was to inform the King and the Council of the Indies of "how I am the descendent of the Inca kings of Peru, and of how Garcilaso de la Vega, my father, one of the first conquerors and settlers of those provinces of Peru and of how he was a citizen and holder of an *encomienda* in the city of Cuzco, and of how he served His Majesty at his own expense on all occasions that were offered, and likewise how I, the said grantor, have served His Majesty in war with four commissions as captain, and likewise how I have served him in the translation of the 'Tres diálogos de amor' of León Hebreo and in the History which I wrote of the discovery that Fernando de Soto made of the kingdom of Florida, and in the 'Comentarios de los Incas, reyes que fueron del Perú,' the first part of which has been published and the rest is being printed."

Garcilaso took the opportunity to reopen the question of a second edition of the *Diálogos de amor;* Burgos y Arellano was to approach the Inquisition for permission to republish (the work had been prohibited in any Spanish translation). If any attempt was made to carry out Garcilaso's wishes, it was too late. He died without the satisfaction of royal recognition.

It is evident that Garcilaso spent considerable time on affairs that had nothing to do with literary matters. But he is remembered today not as the businessman par excellence, not as the heroic captain, not as the godfather to numerous inhabitants of Montilla and Córdoba, but as the author of three books and one translation which have been delighting readers since their first publication.

Executing legal documents and composing formal petitions to King and Council are not normally the exercises that produce a great writer. Somehow, somewhere, Garcilaso, in spite of what would today be considered an entirely inadequate formal education, developed intellectual interests and began to feel the urge to write. The kind of writer a man becomes depends primarily upon his natural talent, but it also depends, among other things, upon the books he reads and the people with whom he associates.

After his death, inventory was made of his property, including his library, which offers some insight into his intellectual interests and some suggestion of the influences which in varying degrees helped form him as a writer.[11] Since the books inventoried were those in his possession at the end of his life, it is more than possible that they represent only a portion of the books he owned and certainly only a portion of the books he read and used. How many books he presented to friends or disposed of in other ways is totally unknown. The copy of Las Casas' treatises, referred to above and which on the testimony of its owner had once belonged to Garcilaso, is missing from the inventory along with other items he must have had. It seems highly unlikely, for example, that the Inca never owned a copy of his illustrious namesake's poems. The inventory lists 188 items, with some duplications, not an extraordinarily large collection for the time, especially for a man whose successful career was made as a writer. Nor is the collection one that could be considered representative of the age. While the entries in the inventory are most inaccurately made, apparently by a clerk—with little talent for the task—who took down short titles from dictation, it is possible to identify a number of them with fair certainty.

The most striking lack in the library is Spanish literature; the only contemporary work listed is the first part of Mateo Alemán's *Guzmán de Alfarache* published in 1599. The only other Spanish literary works were copies of the *Celestina,* the works of the fifteenth-century poet Juan de Mena, and two volumes of the letters of Antonio de Guevara. Some explanation for the lack of prose fiction in an age when Spaniards were extremely fond of that form of literature may be found in Garcilaso's confession in the *Florida*: "Therefore, I can with truth deny that mine is fiction, because all my life—except for good poetry—I have been the enemy of fictions such as the books of chivalry and other like ones. Thanks for this I must give to the illustrious knight Pedro Mejía of Seville, because with a rebuke, which in the *Heroica obra de los Césares* he gave those who occupy themselves in reading and composing such books, he freed me of the love which as a boy I had for them and made me abhor them forever."

It is not surprising, given Garcilaso's strong religious feeling, manifested in all his writings, and the temper of his times, to find a large number of religious books in his collection. These are for the most part either standard religious books, such as the Bible, breviaries and missals or the works of Spanish theologians, the most widely known of whom was Fray Luis de Granada. Two entries are identifiable as copies of the *Index librorum prohibitorum* (the last edition published in Garcilaso's lifetime was that of 1612). Garcilaso's interest in arms and horses is reflected in Jerónimo Carranza's *Destreza de las armas* and Pedro Fernández de Andrada's *De la naturaleza del caballo*. He owned works, unidentifiable by specific titles, by the Spanish Renaissance philosopher Luis Vives and Juan Huarte de San Juan's psychological treatise *Examen de ingenios*. The *Vocabulario de las dos lenguas toscana y castellana* compiled by Cristóbal de las Casas was of obvious utility to Garcilaso in his translating. He had a copy of Francisco de Castro's *De arte rhetorica* published in 1611 and dedicated to Garcilaso. Cosmography (Joannis Sacrobosco's *Esfera* and Jerónimo de Chaves' *Cronografía*), architecture (here the titles are unidentifiable), political philosophy (*De rexis istituzione*, which is probably Juan de Mariana's *De rege et regis institutione*), and science (Alonso de Vera Cruz's *Phisica speculatio*) all interested Garcilaso.

Since he was an historian and in the *Comentarios reales* and in the *Historia general del Perú* he depended heavily upon work already done in the history of the New World, the library contained a considerable number of Spanish historical works. The most important histories from the point of view of the use Garcilaso made of them were José de Acosta's *Historia natural y moral de las Indias*, Juan de Castellanos' *Elegías de varones ilustres de Indias*, Pedro Cieza de León's *Crónica del Perú*, Diego de Fernández' *Crónica del Perú*, Gonzalo Fernández de Oviedo's *Historia General de las Indias*, and Francisco López de Gómara's *Historia General de las Indias*. Other works less directly related to Garcilaso's own writing were the *Corónica llamada de las dos conquistas del reino de Nápoles* by Hernán Pérez del Pulgar and the *Corónica de las tres órdenes y caballerías de Santiago, Calatrava y Alcántara* by Francisco Rades Andrada.

Greek and, especially, Roman writers formed a solid core for the collection. From the entries in the inventory it is in many cases difficult to determine whether the books were in the original languages or whether they were Spanish translations. Garcilaso knew Latin and the presence of an *Arte griega*, that is, a Greek grammar, would indicate that he had some interest in that language, though how extensive his knowledge of it was is impossible to determine. It seems more than likely that he read some of the books in the original. Here again historians are numerous: Caesar, Quintus Curtius Rufus, Flavius Josephus, Lucan, Polybius, Sallust, Suetonius and Thucydides. Aulus Gellius, Cicero, and Plutarch would have appeal because of their relationship to historical writing. Aristotle's *Rhetoric*, the tragedies of Seneca and an unidentified volume of Terence were included. Heliodorus' *Aethiopia* in Spanish translation, Vergil's *Aeneid,* and unspecified works by Ovid rounded out the selection of classical literature.

The strong influence of Italian Renaissance writers in Spain is reflected in Garcilaso's choice of books. It is rather strange that while so little Spanish poetry is listed in the inventory, Italian poets are well represented with Dante's works, Ariosto's *Orlando furioso,* and Boiardo's *Orlando innamorato.* Petrarch's name appears on the list four times and Bembo's twice. Boccaccio, judging from the number of times his name is found, was a favorite author. His *Caída de príncipes, Laberinto de amor* (both apparently in Spanish translation), the *Filocolo,* and two other entries without title are listed. Lodovico Dolce's *Il Palmireno,* Geraldi Cinzio's *Cien novelas,* Alessandro Piccolomini's *Comedias* complete the Italian belles-lettres. Strictly historical works are less numerous than might be expected. Pandolfo Collenuccio's *Compendio de las historias del reino de Nápoles* and a history of Italy which may be the work of Guicciardini, are the only identifiable items in that field. Other Italian writers found are Ficino (perhaps some of his neo-Platonic works), Aldo and Paolo Manuzio, Aretino (*Ragionamenti*), and Tasso (*Lettere familiare*). Castiglione's name appears twice; it may well be that Garcilaso owned both the Italian original and Boscán's Spanish translation of *Il Corteggiano* and used them as model for his own work as a translator. A French version of León Hebreo's *Dialoghi d'amore* suggest that Garcilaso did make comparisons. It would be interesting to know what titles were included in a group indicated only as "Libros italianos."

Not all the books found on Garcilaso's shelves after his death had a direct influence upon his published works, though many of them are cited in the *Florida,* the *Comentarios reales,* and *Historia general del Perú.* The list, so far as identifiable authors and titles are concerned, does not include a number of books that Garcilaso mentions specifically. The most surprising absence, considering the use Garcilaso made of it, is Agustín de Zárate's *Historia del descubrimiento y conquista del Perú*. No indication is found of Jerónimo de Román's *Repúblicas del mundo divididas en XXVII libros*, Pedro Mártir de Anghiera's *Decades de orbe novo*, Gonzalo de Illescas' *Historia pontifical*. Other Spanish works he mentions at some point are Alfonso X's *Crónica general*, Polo de Ondegardo's *Relaciones*, and Alonso de Ercilla y Zúñiga's epic *La araucana*. Garcilaso praised Antonio de Nebrija highly and was clearly familiar with his work, yet none of his books is listed. One Italian, Giovanni Botero, whose *Relaciones universales del mundo* Garcilaso knew, and the French historiographer and political scientist, Jean Bodin, (*De republica libri sex*) are both missing from the list.

Encouragement for Garcilaso to continue his studies and to write must have come first from his acquaintance among the clergy in Montilla. His known literary associations are very few, although in the dedication to the *Diálogos* he indicates that there was a number of "religious and serious persons," whom he does not enumerate because there were too many of them, who had been of considerable assistance to him. He mentions Father Agustín de Herrera, tutor in the household of the Marqués de Priego, Father Jerónimo de Prado, a Jesuit who taught Scripture in Córdoba, Pedro Sánchez de Herrera, particularly singled out as one of Garcilaso's teachers, and the Augustinian, Father Fernando de Zárate, retired professor of theology from the University of Osuna, all of whom had early knowledge of his efforts as a translator and strongly encouraged him to continue in his project.

In Córdoba he was on especially good terms with two Jesuits, Father Francisco de Castro and Father Juan de Pineda. Of the two, Castro was the more literary minded; besides ascetic works, he wrote two rhetorical treatises, *De syllabarum quantitate* and *De arte rhetorica, dialogi quatuor*, this last dedicated with fulsome praise to Garcilaso. Pineda, best known for his commentaries on Job, *Commentariorum in Job libri tredecim*, was to have worked with Garcilaso on an edition of the poems of Garci Sánchez de Badajoz. The work on the poems, particularly on *Las liciones de Job*, prohibited by the Inquisition, was apparently aimed at cleaning them up, or as Garcilaso puts it, "to reduce those divine lessons to their spiritual and divine meaning," a task Garcilaso did not feel qualified to carry out without expert assistance. It was a project Garcilaso was eager to accomplish, but it did not go beyond the stage of discussion because of Garcilaso's other commitments.

The only known letters of Garcilaso are two addressed to Juan

Fernández Franco in 1592 and 1593. Fernández Franco was an antiquarian especially interested in numismatics. He is all but forgotten today, but in the sixteenth century he enjoyed a wide acquaintance among a large group of scholars of similar interests. It is doubtful that he and Garcilaso ever met; the correspondence between them arose evidently from Fernández Franco's having read Garcilaso's translation of León Hebreo. Judging from Garcilaso's reply, Fernández Franco was highly flattering; the Inca writes, "That work [the *Diálogos*], although I put nothing in it but many imperfections, has caused you and other gentlemen to favor me, as you do favor me, without my having any learning but only the perpetual desire for it. Therefore I beg you to treat me like a soldier who, ruined by bad pay, and slow, has become a student." In the second letter, Garcilaso replies to a request for advice from Fernández Franco concerning a projected move to America, this despite the fact that Fernández Franco was over seventy at the time. In his first letter to Fernández Franco, Garcilaso mentions Ambrosio de Morales, another distinguished historian and antiquarian, to whom Garcilaso was indebted for assistance in preparing the translation of the *Diálogos*. Their relationship must have been a close one for Garcilaso says, undoubtedly speaking figuratively, that Morales adopted him as a son.

In Córdoba, Garcilaso was beginning to enjoy a certain renown as an authority on American affairs, particularly, as is natural, in Peruvian matters. Francisco Fernández de Córdoba, in his *Didascalia multiplex*, cites Garcilaso as an authority on the use of iron in the New World and on customs among the Indians of Florida. Another Cordobese, Bernardo de Aldrete, acknowledges in his *Origen y principio de la lengua castellana* that Garcilaso had shown him the manuscript of the *Comentarios reales* and that he had found them a source of information. While Garcilaso does not mention Aldrete by name, they must have been well acquainted since Aldrete was a canon of the collegiate church in Córdoba.[12] Another famous name in Spanish literature not mentioned by Garcilaso is that of Luis de Góngora y Argote. There is no indication as to what their personal dealings were except for certain business affairs connected with the estate of their common kinswoman, Doña Luisa Ponce de León. It is just possible that Garcilaso, whose taste in poetry was evidently very conservative, found that he had little in common with the great baroque poet.

In the last years of his life, Garcilaso's relations with the clergy of Córdoba were particularly close; indeed he was one of their number. In a document of 1612, he is referred to as "Garzia Laso Ynga de la Bega, clérigo." Just what his status was is nowhere made clear; it is doubtful that he was ordained a priest, more likely he was in minor orders.

In 1612 Garcilaso, who had considered himself an old man since the age of fifty, began to make provision for his burial place. He was content with no ordinary grave, but purchased a chapel in the great cathedral of Córdoba as a fitting site for the tomb of a descendant of kings, warriors, and poets. Much of his energy in these late years was spent in arranging the repair and decoration of the chapel and in providing the endowment required to maintain it properly. The contract Garcilaso signed on July 9, 1614, for a large crucifix reveals that, although his physical strength was failing, he was still able to protect himself in business affairs. The crucifix was to be delivered by Christmas of that year, the materials and form were specified, and further it was agreed that the price would be determined upon its completion by two people, one chosen by Garcilaso and one by the sculptor, but that in no case should the Inca be required to pay more than a hundred ducats.

Occasionally, even in notarial documents, there appears a hint of something more than cold legal proceedings; Garcilaso's last recorded business transaction was on August 20, 1615. The paper was signed for Garcilaso by one of the witnesses, "because he said that he cannot sign because of his trembling hand."

On April 18, 1616, when Garcilaso was in his final illness, he had his will drawn up. It too was signed by proxy. Five codicils were added, the last on the day of his death, April 22. He was buried in his own chapel where two memorial tablets were placed. The first, on the Gospel side, reads:

The Inca Garcilaso de la Vega, a renowned man, worthy of perpetual memory, illustrious in blood, accomplished in letters, valiant in arms, son of Garcilaso de la Vega of the houses of the Dukes of Feria and Infantado and of Elizabeth Palla sister of Huaina Capac last Emperor of the Indies. He commented upon Florida, translated Leon Hebreo and composed the Comentarios reales.

The stone on the Epistle side reads:

He lived in Córdoba with great religion, he died exemplarily, he endowed this chapel, he was buried in it, he dedicated his wealth to the suffrage of the souls in Purgatory, the Dean and Chapter of this Holy Church are perpetual patrons. He died April 22, 1616. Pray God for his soul.

CHAPTER 3

The Diálogos de amor

GARCILASO'S initiation into the literary world was not through any original work but through his translation from Italian of León Hebreo's *Dialoghi d'amore*. The translation was published in 1590 in Madrid by Pedro Madrigal, one of the capital's most successful publishers. It bore, as was usual for the time, a long title: *La traducción del indio de los tres diálogos de amor de León Hebreo hecha de Italiano en español por Garcilaso Inca de la Vega natural de la gran ciudad del Cuzco, cabeza de los reinos y provincias del Perú. Dirigidos a la Sacra Católica Real Majestad del Rey Don Felipe Nuestro Señor* (The Indian's translation of the three dialogues on love of León Hebreo done from Italian into Spanish by Garcilaso Inca de la Vega native of the great city of Cuzco, capital of the kingdoms and provinces of Peru. Directed to the Sacred Catholic Royal Majesty of King Philip Our Lord).

The translation, judging from Garcilaso's letter to Maximiliano de Austria, was virtually complete by September 18, 1586. Maximiliano had heard Garcilaso's work praised and had expressed a wish to see it; Garcilaso replied with a request for Maximiliano's aid in his proposal to dedicate his work to the King. Maximiliano did not receive the manuscript until June 17, 1587, because Garcilaso had difficulty finding help in making a copy. He writes on March 12, 1587, that it was impossible to find good copyists in Montilla; the best one he was able to find made so poor a job of it that Garcilaso had to recopy it himself. Maximiliano was apparently favorably impressed and used his good offices. The book appeared with the dedication to the King which Garcilaso had forehandedly prepared in January, 1586.[1]

At no time does Garcilaso indicate who introduced him to Hebreo's book or when he first read it and found it much to his liking. It may well be doubted that Garcilaso had become interested in the Jewish philosopher before his abortive attempt at a military career, but it is certain that the work was begun and finished while he was still in Montilla. In his letter to Juan Fernández Franco he remarks that he began to translate the dialogues to fill the leisure time he had there. He reveals something more in his address to Maximiliano de

CARNEGIE LIBRARY
LIVINGSTONE COLLEGE
SALISBURY, N. C. 28144

Austria, prefixed to the dialogues. As he read the text and became entranced with its doctrine, he began to read more slowly and carefully and at last started to translate it bit by bit for his own benefit and entertainment. After he had spent some days in this pastime, he showed his work to some of his friends who urged him to persevere in his undertaking, to give it his best attention for, as they assured him, it would be well received. What had been begun as recreation was soon to become a task that required great discipline, though even with all the hard work the translation cost him, it probably never lost its intrinsic appeal.

In the prologue to the *Historia general del Perú*, Garcilaso gives an anecdote relating to his translation that reveals considerable about himself. A certain dignitary of the cathedral of Córdoba had seen the work and expressed a desire to meet the translator. Garcilaso, as he reports it, dared not appear before so grand a person, but after much urging did pay a call upon his admirer who "did me great favor in everything, although he was in bed swollen with gout, and the first words with which he greeted me were these, 'An Antarctic, born in the New World, down there under our hemisphere and who drank in with his mother's milk the general language of the Indians of Peru, why should he become an interpreter between Italians and Spaniards? And once he presumed to become one, why did he not take just any book and not the one that the Italians most esteemed and the Spaniards knew least?' I replied to him that it had been soldierly temerity, for they accomplish their greatest deeds that way, and if they emerge victorious they are considered valiant and if they die in the attempt they are considered mad."

It was something different from soldierly temerity, although that may have helped, that set him off on the career which was to bring him in Spain the recognition he so fervently desired. It is in some ways extraordinary that Garcilaso should have chosen this particular text; the question posed by the ecclesiastic was pertinent. The *Dialoghi d'amore* have received great praise as a neo-Platonic document and there is general agreement that Hebreo's investigation of the nature and effect of love is one of the very few real contributions made to philosophy in the Renaissance, yet no modern philosopher has produced an adequate analysis of the work.[2]

I *León Hebreo and His* Dialoghi

The known facts of the life of León Hebreo are few. Born probably in Lisbon between 1460 and 1470, the son of Isaac Abarbanel, he was given the name Jehudah; the name León was undoubtedly adopted later because of the association with the lion of Judah. His father was a distinguished physician, counsellor to Alfonso V of Portugal and, after 1484, to Ferdinand the Catholic of Spain. León Hebreo followed his father's profession and is said by some to have been personal physician to Isabel and Ferdinand. In 1492, when the Jews were expelled from Spain, the family found refuge first in Naples, later in Genoa. In Italy he was the personal friend of Pico della Mirandola and probably of other humanists of the time. The *Dialoghi d'amore* were probably written about 1502, though they were not published until 1535. He was reputedly the author of elegies written in Hebrew and of a treatise on the harmony of the heavens, no longer extant. The original language of the *Dialoghi* is unknown; claims have been made by eager Hispanophiles that they were composed in Spanish but there is no evidence to support the theory. Garcilaso was of the opinion that the work was originally written in Italian, an opinion shared by most modern scholars.

Of the three dialogues that constitute the book, the first deals with the nature and essence of love, the second with its universality, and the third with its origin. The interlocutors are Filón and Sofía whose names indicate what they symbolize, love or appetite and knowledge or wisdom. The philosophical discourses which fill the dialogues are serious, but they take place under circumstances which at times add a tone of lightheartedness to the discussion—Filón is courting Sofía.

The argument begins with a distinction between love and desire; love is for the thing possessed, desire for the thing not possessed. Nothing that does not exist either actually or potentially can be either loved or desired and knowledge must precede either love or desire. The good is desired by all; therefore the thing loved or desired must have being, it must be true and it must be good. There are two kinds of love: real love for something definitely known, and imagined love for those desired things whose nature is understood in the imagination. Some things, like truth and wisdom, are both loved and desired. Some things are loved and not desired, like all good things that are possessed. Some things are desired but not loved; that is, health, children not yet born, and other things that do not have actual existence. Love and desire may be felt for three kinds of things: the useful, the delightful, and the honest, which is equated with virtue and wisdom. The love of the useful—riches, worldly possessions—never satisfies the possessor. The love of the delightful, the pleasurable, is broader and more universal that the love of the useful, but the love of the honest exceeds either of the other two. The end of honest love is the perfection of the intellective soul. Health, children, power, honor, glory, friendship move men to love or desire, but love of God is the beginning, middle, and end of all honest acts. Human love for God ought to exceed all other honest love; the extent of love for the divine depends upon the capacity of the mind to encompass the greatness of God, in whom all wisdom and virtue exist in perfection. Perfect happiness consists not of knowledge, nor of the love which follows knowledge, but rather of the union of the human mind with the divine.

If today the dialogues are generally read only by the curious few who see them primarily as having historical importance, their acceptance in the sixteenth century was quite different. The book went through at least ten Italian editions within the century, it was translated into Latin in 1564, into French in 1559. In Italy the crowd of writers who produced neo-Platonic treatises on love are almost without exception indebted to León Hebreo.

II *Garcilaso's Translation*

Garcilaso's translation of the dialogues was not their first Spanish version. Two translations of which he seems to have been unaware had appeared before Garcilaso's. The first anonymous one was published in 1568 in Venice, the second by Carlos Montesa was published at Zaragoza in 1582. The desirability of a third translation within so short a time might be questioned, but even if Garcilaso had been aware of the other two, he was justified in publishing his own version. As has already been indicated, the first edition was exhausted fairly soon and Garcilaso began to think of a second. Its success was undoubtedly due to the popularity of the subject matter but Garcilaso's own contribution was not at all negligible. Menéndez y Pelayo, the nineteenth-century dean of Spanish letters who was by no means always so kind to Garcilaso, judges Garcilaso's work to be far superior to that of his predecessors.

Garcilaso's plans for a second edition of the dialogues may have been impeded by the Inquisition. It has been erroneously stated that the Holy Office forbade Garcilaso's translation specifically and Garcilaso himself gives the impression that this work was singled out for particular censure. The dialogues, in all editions and in all languages, were entered in the *Index librorum prohibitorum et expurgatorum* of 1612. They were listed in the second class which included works of certain authors that were prohibited or to which words of caution or explanation were to be added. In his remarks concerning a possible second edition, Garcilaso says nothing about emending the text to take care of the objections of the Inquisition, whatever they were.

Garcilaso's good translation is the result of his learning and linguistic skill; it is also the result of his attitude toward the work he is translating and his idea of a translator's responsibility. In his letter to Maximiliano de Austria, he warns his reader that the dialogues must be read "with no ordinary attention because it seems that the intention of the author was to write, not for the careless, but for those who go along philosophizing with him. . . . To see that he wrote, in such common language with such inventiveness, not for the common crowd, is to esteem him highly." Garcilaso's approach to the translator's task is a sound one: "For my part I can affirm that the typographical errors cost me much work, and much more my attempt to interpret it faithfully with the same words that its author used in Italian, without adding other superfluous ones, for it is sufficient that it be understood with the ones he used and not with more. For to add to them would be to make its doctrine very common, which is what he most avoided, and to corrupt the gravity and composure of his speech."

What is significant about the dialogues in relation to the Inca is not that it represents original work; for the intellectual effort in formulating the concepts and in expounding them Garcilaso can claim no credit. The intellectual exercise for him consisted of the problem of converting as closely as possible all the thought of the original into another language, a task that demands constant interpretation of the first text. To accomplish it, the good translator must have excellent command of both languages involved, and equally important, he must have understanding of the material he is translating. The quality of the finished product as an example of the translator's art will depend upon the degree to which the translator has control of his materials.

Garcilaso himself says that he found the philosophy of the *Diálogos de amor* congenial. The extent to which neo-Platonism dominated his thought is a theme that demands careful study. It can only be suggested here, but even discarding Garcilaso's statements about the attractiveness of Hebreo's work, there is still evidence that the neo-Platonic view of the universe was strongly influential in his writing. It is to be noted that in his library he had works by Ficino,

Bembo, Castiglione, and Tasso, all of whom in one way or another expound the neo-Platonic doctrine. The influence of that doctrine will be seen in the application Garcilaso makes of the use of myth, particularly the myth of Jupiter as the loving conqueror recounted in the second dialogue, in the idea of progression from barbaric, pagan ignorance to knowledge of the true God, in the spirit of order and harmony that pervades his work, in the idea of the divine will at work in the world.

CHAPTER 4

La Florida del Inca

G ARCILASO'S second published book and first original work appeared in Lisbon in 1605. Published by Pedro Crasbeeck, it bore the title *La Florida del Inca. Historia del adelantado Hernando de Soto, gobernador y capitán general del reino de la Florida, y de otros heroicos caballeros españoles e indios, escrita por el Inca Garcilaso de la Vega, capitán de Su Majestad, natural de la gran ciudad del Cozco, cabeza de los reinos y provincias del Perú* (The Florida of the Inca. History of the Adelantado Hernando de Soto, Governor and Captain General of the Kingdom of Florida, and of other heroic Spanish and Indian cavaliers, written by the Inca Garcilaso de la Vega, His Majesty's Captain, native of the great city of Cuzco, capital of the kingdoms and provinces of Peru).

I *Résumé*

The *Florida* is not a day-by-day account of de Soto's march, but a well-organized narrative divided into six books, one for each year of the expedition. Books II and V are each in two parts. Garcilaso says he divided Book II so that it would not be so long as to tire the reader; there were more events to record in that year than in any of the others. The division in Book V was made to separate the events of that year up to the death of de Soto from those that occurred when Luis Moscoso de Alvarado assumed command.

In the fifteen chapters of Book I which serve as general introduction to the history, Garcilaso relates how the restless de Soto, unwilling to settle down to a quiet life in Spain where he might enjoy the wealth he brought back from Peru, petitioned Charles V for permission to undertake the conquest of Florida at his own expense. After locating the area geographically as well as he could, since in his day its limits were not fixed, Garcilaso reviews the previous attempts to explore it with brief accounts of the expeditions of Ponce de León, Lucas Vásquez de Ayllón and Pánfilo de Narváez. De Soto's fleet sailed from San Lúcar de Barrameda in April, 1538, and in due course reached Santiago de Cuba and from there sailed to Havana. Final organization of the expedition and de Soto's duties as governor of Cuba delayed matters so that it was something over a year after leaving Spain that the expedition departed Cuba for Florida.

With the first part of Book II, consisting of thirty chapters, the real narrative begins with the arrival of de Soto on the coast of Florida, apparently at Tampa Bay. A lengthy digression relates the story of Juan Ortiz, a member of Narváez' expedition who had spent ten years among the Indians. Although he had nearly forgotten his mother tongue, Ortiz joined the expedition as interpreter. Leaving Pedro Calderón behind to guard the ships and supplies, de Soto began his march inland toward the north and east. After a difficult crossing of a great swamp, the expedition moved on through the territories of Acuera, a decidedly unfriendly chief, and of Ocali until they reached the village of Ochile belonging to Vitachuco. The latter appeared at first friendly but secretly plotted to wipe out the Spanish force. De Soto received timely warning and captured Vitachuco along with nine hundred Indians who were made slaves of the Spaniards as a warning to other unfriendly tribes. Vitachuco was himself killed when he attacked de Soto. After a riot of the slaves, during which they were all slain, de Soto moved on to Osachile.

The twenty-five chapters of the second part of Book II take the expedition from Osachile to the province of Apalachee. The passage was extremely difficult because of the swampy nature of the land and the constant attacks of the Indians. A scouting party sent out to find the best way back to the sea, after being led astray by a treacherous guide, at last came to the site of Narváez' abandoned camp near Apalachee Bay. De Soto decided to winter in Apalachee because of its abundant provisions. A band of thirty led by Juan de Añasco was sent off to summon Calderón. A major portion of the book is filled with the description of the hazardous trip of the thirty back to Calderón's camp and the equally difficult march of Calderón and his men to Apalachee. Añasco returned by sea with two brigantines. While in winter camp, de Soto heard rumors of a province called Cofachiqui where there were great quantities of gold, silver and pearls.

Book III's thirty-nine chapters relate the march northward from Apalachee into what is now southern Georgia. At Cofa they encountered friendly Indians and were able to rest before pressing on to Cofaqui where they were also received affably. The chief at Cofaqui supplied both food and escort for the trip into neighboring Cofachiqui. A hard trip during which even their native guides became lost brought the Spaniards to a meeting with the Lady of Cofachiqui. The expected riches were a disappointment—copper and iron pyrites instead of gold and silver—though they did find a great quantity of pearls. The Spaniards moved on to Xuala, in northwestern South Carolina, and from there north and west into Tennessee, then south into Alabama where they encountered the fierce chief Tascaluza. The next stop was Mauvila where Tascaluza resolved to wipe out the expedition. A night battle ensued; the Spaniards emerged victorious but with heavy losses. De Soto became aware of discontent among his men, some of whom were planning an insurrection as soon as the army reached the coast. To forestall it de Soto marched to the west instead of continuing toward the south. At the end of 1540 they had moved into Mississippi.

Book IV, containing sixteen chapters, opens with a Spanish attack upon the fortress of Alibamo. Since the army was suffering seriously from lack of salt, the expedition became as much a search for that necessity as for gold. After Alibamo, they marched to the Mississippi which they crossed on barges. Aided by the friendly chief Casquin, de Soto moved into the territory of Capaha, a long-time enemy of Casquin. One of de Soto's nobler accomplishments was to make peace between the two. The expedition moved through Arkansas, stopping at Quiguate and Colima. They wintered at Utiangue.

The first part of Book V, eight chapters, marks the climax of the *Florida*. In April of 1542, the expedition left Utiangue for Naguatex and Guancane, at which point de Soto decided to turn back to the Mississippi where he intended to found a settlement. His strength was failing and he was eager to take the first step toward establishing a Spanish colony. According to Garcilaso, de Soto fell ill of a fever on June 20, 1542, and realized that he would not recover from it. He appointed Luis de Moscoso de Alvarado to succeed him as commander. After his death, his men buried him at night lest the Indians profane the grave. It soon became evident that the Indians knew where de Soto was buried. The Spaniards then decided that the Mississippi was the proper grave for him.

The last part of Book V, consisting of fifteen chapters, is the story of the abandonment of de Soto's project. The expedition turned westward, thinking to meet other Spaniards who were exploring from Mexico. After they had gone some distance into Texas, they concluded that they had made a false start and would do better to return to the Mississippi. By now the army was exhausted physically and spiritually and found the trip back to the river far more difficult than any of their other marches. The winter and spring were spent in the construction of seven boats to carry them to the sea.

Twenty-two chapters in Book VI recount the passage of the army down the Mississippi, constantly harassed by attacks of the Indians, to the coast where they engaged in a final battle before taking to the sea. A long journey along the coast at last brought them to Pánuco in Mexico; from there they went to Mexico City where they gave a full report to the viceroy.

II   *Genesis of the* Florida

The appearance of the *Florida* in 1605 marked the end of a project begun at least eighteen years earlier. When Garcilaso wrote to Maximiliano de Austria on March 12, 1587, concerning the dedication of the *Diálogos de amor*, he referred to his history of Florida which was at that time one-fourth finished. This would mean that he probably started writing the book no later than 1586, and perhaps earlier. At the end of December, 1592, he wrote in his letter to Juan Fernández Franco that he had the history of Florida finished but that he was having trouble again finding copyists. He hoped to be able to send Fernández Franco a complete copy the following year for criticism and suggestions. He also said that before his death in 1591, Ambrosio de Morales had seen and commented upon a fourth of the work, undoubtedly the same portion referred to in the letter to Maximiliano.

Like all his other prefaces, the proem to the *Florida* addressed to the reader offers considerable insight into the personality of Garcilaso. After discussing the sources he used for the book and his purpose in writing it, Garcilaso disavows any expectation of material reward for his long labors and, in an obvious reference to his lack of success in his petitions to the King, remarks that he long since gave up all attempts and dismissed hope because of the contrariness of his fortune. His ill usage at Fortune's hands was not without some benefit; in a passage reminiscent of Horace and Fray Luis de León, he confesses, "Although, looking upon it dispassionately, I must thank her greatly for having treated me badly, because, if she had shared her goods and favors generously with me, perhaps I would have set out on other roads and paths which might have carried me to worse precipices or might have annihilated me in that great sea with its waves and storms, as she nearly always destroys those whom she has most favored and raised up in the places of eminence of the world. Since I have had experience of her disfavor and persecution, she has forced me to flee her and to hide myself in the port and shelter of the disillusioned, which are the corners of solitude and poverty, where, consoled and satisfied with my scanty means, I lead, thanks to the King of Kings and Lord of Lords, a life quiet and peaceful, more envied by the rich than envious of them."

Clearly Garcilaso had not given up all hope of favor either from Fortune or from some other source, but his words have the ring of sincerity when he says that he derives more satisfaction and recreation for the soul from his writing than from the pursuit of wealth and that it is his hope that his books will bring him honor and fame.

The initial inspiration for the *Florida*, Garcilaso announces in his proem, came from conversations he had with a man—a great friend of his—a member of de Soto's expedition, who related the many great deeds accomplished during the exploration both by Spaniards and by Indians. Garcilaso felt it was most unfortunate that such heroic works should remain forgotten, that future generations should have no adequate record of the glorious but ill-fated effort made by de Soto and his men. He had a twofold obligation in preserving the story: a duty to Spain because of his father, and a duty to the noble Indians of Florida because of his mother. He urged his unnamed friend to join him in the task of writing the history. Garcilaso, since he had no claims to knowledge either of Florida or of the expedition, was to serve as scribe.

III *Garcilaso's Purpose*

After the early explorations of Ponce de León, Pánfilo de Narváez and de Soto, no serious attempt had been made by Spain to colonize the peninsula. The descriptions of the glories of Florida, so named not because of its vegetation but because of its discovery on Easter, aroused Garcilaso's interest, and the thought of a land so rich in potential if not in actuality, unexploited and probably eventually to be lost through neglect, stirred feelings of national pride in the heart of the mestizo. His purpose, then, in writing the *Florida* was to honor the heroes of the expedition and, even more important, to stir the hearts of Spaniards to make an effort to complete the conquest of the land and to fill it with Spanish settlers. He was of the opinion that the land could be made even more productive than it was by the introduction of new plants and animals from Spain and other parts of the world.

Repeatedly in his narrative, Garcilaso returns to the theme of the necessity for action in Florida. In Chapter 9 of Book VI he regrets that de Soto and his men were so intent upon the search for gold and silver, neither of which they found, that they did not devote themselves properly to gathering information necessary for colonization. That apparent lack of precious metals should be no cause for discouragement, says Garcilaso, because they were sure to be found since there had as yet been no part of the New World thoroughly explored that had not produced treasure. The explorers and colonists need not be without sources of wealth before the discovery of the mines that undoubtedly existed; pearls were to be found in great supply, the large number of mulberry trees would support silk production, greater abundance of pasture and more fertile land could hardly be desired. The conquest of Florida, he asserts, would be easier than that of many other parts of the New World where Spaniards had extended themselves. Transportation from Spain was easy —one ship could make two trips a year, horses and other supplies could come easily from the Caribbean islands and from Mexico. His enthusiasm for the undertaking is so intense that he wishes he had had the opportunity to participate in it himself. Its accomplishment, alas, would have to await someone more fortunate.

Economic opportunities for Spain and for individual Spaniards as a result of the colonization of Florida clearly seemed to Garcilaso one of the most effective arguments he could use with the King and his subjects to stir them to action. While Garcilaso makes no direct mention of it, political advantages were also to be gained from Spanish settlement of Florida. Garcilaso could hardly have been unaware of the threats from France and England, yet his only recognition of the danger is two brief statements, one to the effect that it was to be feared that Spain's neighboring countries "infected with the abominable heresies of these unhappy times" would succeed in gaining a foothold and would corrupt the innocent natives (VI, 9); the other statement is in reference to Pedro Menéndez de Avilés who made three trips to Florida between 1563 and 1568 to drive out French corsairs who were attempting to settle there. The French expeditions were led by Jean Ribaut and René de Laudonnière who sought to establish Huguenot colonies on the St. Johns River. Menéndez de Avilés wiped out the French settlement and established one of his own, St. Augustine. No attempt was made to move inland and the coastal settlement remained vulnerable to attack from the sea. The most serious attack upon it was by Sir Francis Drake who all but destroyed the town in 1586.

Far more important to Garcilaso than economic and political advantages was the responsibility of Spain for the conversion of the Indians of Florida. In the proem he takes his stand unequivocally: "For certainly, confessing the whole truth, I say that no other purpose moved me to labor and to write it except the desire that the Christian religion be extended throughout the length and breadth of that land." As he makes clear when he writes the history of Peru, where Spanish conquest and its attendant missionary activities were accomplished fact, the greatest contribution Spain made in the New World was to bring the Gospel to the Indians. Like the Incas, the Indians of Florida were, according to Garcilaso, particularly ready to accept Christianity because of the very few pagan ceremonies and abuses they would have to abandon.

The final chapter of the *Florida* is a roll of the religious who lost their lives in Florida before 1568. Garcilaso closes his work with a fervent appeal, "I trust in God that their blood is crying out for and demanding, not vengeance like that of Abel, but mercy like that of Christ our Lord so that those gentiles may come into knowledge of His Eternal Majesty, under the obedience of Our Mother, the Holy Roman Church."

In view of Garcilaso's identifying himself as an Indian, and in view of his treatment of the Peruvian Indians in the *Comentarios reales,* one may suspect still another motive behind the *Florida;* that is, to present the Indians in a favorable light, to counteract the idea of a barbaric people incapable of human behavior. Garcilaso takes pains to show that basically the Indians behave in much the same way their Spanish visitors did. When it becomes necessary for him to report Indian cruelty, treachery or other unpleasant manifestations of the human spirit, he does so, but balances such reports with incidents that show Spaniards capable of similar acts. The Spaniards often suffer from comparison with Indians like the chieftain Mucozo who displayed great nobility of mind and spirit. It was necessary, if Spain was to undertake the Christianization of the Indians, to demonstrate that the Indians were worthy; there was also the matter of Garcilaso's personal pride that no doubt influenced his portrayal of the native culture.

IV *Gonzalo Silvestre*

Garcilaso says that his principal source of information for the *Florida* was the unidentified *hidalgo* who had accompanied de Soto. There is today no question of the identity of the individual; he was Gonzalo Silvestre.[1] Why Garcilaso did not identify him, as he did his other sources, must remain a mystery but it seems unlikely that Garcilaso, who is normally scrupulous in such matters, concealed the name for reasons of his own. It is perhaps not too much to assume that Garcilaso was rather respecting the wishes of Silvestre, though modesty seems not to have been his outstanding characteristic.

Suspicion that Silvestre was the anonymous friend was first aroused by the prominent role he played in the narrative published by Garcilaso. Silvestre's activities, which are slighted by other writers, are reported in considerable detail in Garcilaso's account. De Soto remains the leader of the expedition, but at times one could be forgiven for assuming that Silvestre was his second in command. The incidents in which Silvestre is the central figure, though largely trivial, show him to good advantage. He was capable of great and noble deeds. His most spectacular performance bears a striking resemblance to passages in those lying histories, the books of chivalry, so deplored by Garcilaso. Four Spaniards, Silvestre among them, were attacked by a particularly fierce Indian whose mighty arm and heavy battle-ax laid low the first three of his enemies. Silvestre was another kind of foe, however, and dodging the Indian's attack, he slashed the Indian across the forehead, face and chest, lopping off his left hand all with the same blow. The Indian made one more attempt, but in vain; Silvestre slashed crosswise through the waist so swiftly and neatly that "the Indian remained standing and said to the Spaniard, 'Peace be with you.' And, having spoken these words, he fell dead cut in two." (IV, 14) Silvestre's blow is noteworthy; no less so are the surprising words of the Indian.

Internal evidence in such problems of identification is good and useful, but it is often not decisive. In the case of Silvestre and Garcilaso, there is sufficient external evidence of their relationship as to leave little if any question of the role of Silvestre in the composition of the *Florida*.

Gonzalo Silvestre was a native of the town of Herrera de Alcántara in Extremadura, born about 1518 since in the *Florida* he is described as being but little more than twenty in 1539.[2] He was one of the eight hundred who enlisted for the expedition to Florida. After the survivors of de Soto's force reached Mexico, some of them returned to Spain, while others were tempted by the possibility of further adventure and the hope of greater wealth in Peru. Silvestre was one of the latter. The course of his life there, although filled with activity, was not prosperous. He became involved in the civil wars, took part in the great battle of Huarina on the side of the King's supporters, and continued to serve with the armies that were ultimately victorious. Unlike Garcilaso's father, who was able to maintain his standing in spite of his frequent alliances with rebels, Silvestre received no satisfactory reward for his service against Gonzalo Pizarro. He had no better fortune seeking favor after the rebellion of Hernández Girón in 1554. With a number of other discontented veterans, he went to Lima to press his claims before the viceroy. The appeal was not successful; in fact, it produced exactly the opposite of the desired effect. According to Silvestre, he aroused the viceroy's wrath because he refused to marry one of the prostitutes sent over from Spain. As a result, he and several others were forced to leave the colony and return to Spain.

He was in Madrid when Garcilaso came to the capital; Silvestre was no more successful than Garcilaso in his pretensions. Even though he did not obtain what he wanted, he was apparently respected as being well informed and trustworthy; Garcilaso says in the proem to the *Florida* that he was often consulted by the Council of the Indies on matters concerning the expedition to Florida and other campaigns in which Silvestre had participated. There is no certain indication of when the collaboration between Garcilaso and Silvestre began, but it may have been during the time when both were in Madrid. The French intrusions into Florida must have been a topic of conversation in the Court and it is quite possible that Garcilaso's acquaintance with Silvestre, combined with the news of the day, suggested to Garcilaso the possibility of writing a history of the colony based upon the account of an eyewitness to the most extensive exploration of the area that had been made to that date.

It would appear that Garcilaso began to gather his materials from Silvestre before 1570. In the proem he says that while both parties to the undertaking were eager to see it completed, their efforts were frequently interrupted, either by the war in which Garcilaso took part or by long periods of absence of one or the other. Thus more than twenty years were consumed in the project. Garcilaso was not always as precise in his chronology as one could wish; the statement about the twenty-year period does not help much to fix either the date of the beginning or of the termination of the book. In the course of those twenty years, Garcilaso began to worry lest either he or Silvestre would die before the work was done. Neither could finish without the other; Silvestre would lack someone to spur him on and to act as his scribe, and Garcilaso would lack the necessary information. With this in mind, Garcilaso decided to put an end to all the interruptions by giving up "the comfort I enjoyed in the town where I was living and go to his where we devoted ourselves carefully and diligently to writing all that happened on this expedition, from its beginning to its end for the honor and fame of the Spanish nation which has done such great things in the New World, and no less for that of the Indians who in the history will show themselves worthy of the same honor," as he wrote to his friend Fernández Franco.

The town in which Silvestre was living was Las Posadas, a few miles to the southwest of Córdoba. The lacunae in the Montilla documents relating to Garcilaso are no doubt due in part to his visits to Las Posadas. He was definitely spending time in that town in 1587 and 1589 as is shown in the preliminary letters of the *Diálogos de amor*. Garcilaso's acquaintance with Silvestre, which dated from 1552 developed into a close friendship; Garcilaso was named one of the executors of his will. Garcilaso gives the date of their first acquaintance in his last known legal document, a memorial executed on the day of his death, which he wished to be considered a part of his will. The first item in the document is a statement concerning debts owed him by Silvestre and consequently by Silvestre's heir. He also reveals that Silvestre was a great spender and that since the beginning of their relationship Silvestre had been constantly in his debt.[3]

It is in the *Comentarios reales* that Garcilaso names Silvestre as a source of information and makes indirect acknowledgment of his indebtedness to him. In Chapter 29 of Book IX he says, "When I told this same story to Gonzalo Silvestre, of whom we made lengthy mention in our history of Florida and will do so again in this one if we reach his time, he told me that it was not surprising." This would indicate that Silvestre was a source of information not only for the *Florida* but for the *Comentarios reales* as well.

V *Other Sources*

The oral accounts of Silvestre formed the basis for the *Florida*, as Garcilaso recognizes in the proem and again in various passages, but there were two other, written sources which Garcilaso used to supplement Silvestre. Both of these were reports of members of the expedition; the first was by Alonso de Carmona, a native of the Villa de Priego, who after the Florida venture had gone to Peru where he spent a number of years before returning to Spain. According to Garcilaso, Carmona wrote the account of his travels in America simply for the pleasure it gave him to recall the past. He sent a copy of his work to Garcilaso, not knowing that he was engaged in writing on the same topic. His section on Florida, Garcilaso says, was brief and put together in haphazard fashion, but nonetheless useful.

The second manuscript, another short and disorderly narrative, was written by Juan Coles on the suggestion and encouragement of a Franciscan friar, Pedro Aguado. Aguado was making a collection of accounts of Spanish explorations, particularly those in the Caribbean area, all written by participants in the various actions. The collection of manuscripts had been left with a printer in Córdoba, unrevised and all but forgotten. Among them, Garcilaso found Coles' papers, damaged by moths and mice. Both these written accounts came to his attention after he had completed his own history. Garcilaso thought it best to rewrite, inserting in the proper places the very words of Carmona and Coles "so that by presenting two witnesses who confirm my author, it will be seen that all three accounts are the same."

Questions have been raised concerning Garcilaso's possible use of three other reports of de Soto's expedition. The first of these was published anonymously in Evora, Portugal, in 1557: *True account of the hardships which the governor don Fernando de Soto and certain Portuguese gentlemen suffered in the discovery of the province of Florida. Now newly done by a gentleman of Elvas.*[4] Rodrigo Rangel, a member of de Soto's company, kept an account of the expedition, which was incorporated into Gonzalo Fernández de Oviedo's *Historia general y natural de las Indias,* and Luis Hernández de Biedma, the factor of the expedition, also wrote his version of events. This account was apparently submitted to the Council of the Indies in 1544. Garcilaso says in the proem that one of the royal chroniclers had compared the *Florida* with an account given to the viceroy of New Spain, Antonio de Mendoza, by a member of the expedition, and had found Garcilaso's work to be true and in accord with that report. The royal chronicler is not identified; he may have been Ambrosio de Morales who is known to have seen at least a part of the *Florida* but who died before the work was completed. Antonio de Herrera is a more likely candidate; since he had access to royal papers, it is probable that the account by Hernández de Biedma, given to Mendoza in Mexico, was the one with which the *Florida* was compared.

Whether or not Garcilaso did use one or all of these three in the composition of the *Florida* is still an unanswered question, and one that is likely to remain so. It is not at all certain that he even knew of their existence; at no point does he mention them, although he does refer to Hernández de Biedma, but only in his role of factor, not as author. So far as can be determined, Garcilaso is always careful to acknowledge any literary debt. A certain similarity in all accounts must be expected, as Garcilaso found when he compared the stories of Carmona, Coles and Silvestre, because events observable by anyone present occurred in definite places and in definite order. If Garcilaso did use sources other than those he cites specifically, it could be that they served as aids in placing the events in their correct order. Certainly the *Florida* bears the mark of Garcilaso's personality, and any debt he may have owed is overshadowed by his originality.

VI The Florida *as History*

Garcilaso wrote the *Florida* with a particular purpose, or purposes, a circumstance that inevitably had an effect upon the form the work assumed. No attempt is made to conceal the fact that the final goal of the book was to produce action in others. But for all his concern about the goals he hoped to achieve, Garcilaso is even more concerned about the quality of his work as history. Whatever doubts have arisen in the minds of later generations about the accuracy of the *Florida,* Garcilaso himself was persuaded that what he wrote was in fact the truth about de Soto's venture into the wilds of Florida and neighboring territories. He is completely convinced of the accuracy and veracity of his main witness: "My greatest care was to write the things that are related in it as they are and as they happened, because, it being my principal intention that that land be gained for the purpose already mentioned, I tried to draw out from the one who gave me the account everything that he saw. He was a noble hidalgo who prided himself in telling the truth in everything. As I have seen, the Royal Council of the Indies many times has called upon him as a trustworthy man to verify things which took place during this expedition as well as on others in which he took part." (Proem) Garcilaso protests that he is not writing fiction, indeed he could not do so if he presented the history to the whole Spanish nation which would be justifiably angered if he falsified the account.

With the twenty-seventh chapter of the second part of Book II, Garcilaso interrupts his narrative, after recording a particularly eloquent oration delivered by four young Indians, to reaffirm the good faith of his informant. While Garcilaso knew, as all his readers do, that the words in which the noble thoughts of the Indians are expressed were in fact his own and not literally those of the Indians, he thought he was giving a faithful version. Some doubt as to how far the imagination of his public could be strained caused him to devote the whole chapter to answering anticipated criticisms.

Garcilaso recognizes that the Indians of the New World were generally considered simple people, little better than animals, and therefore incapable of any of the lofty words and deeds he attributes to them. It will be charged, he fears, that his description of Indian behavior is designed to praise and exaggerate the good qualities of his own nation. He flatly denies that the popular idea is a correct one and cites Spanish authority in his own support. So far as any exaggeration and falsification is concerned, he protests that exactly the contrary is true. He had such an abundance of true episodes to recount and fit into his history that he had no need to invent anything. Returning to his original point, the authenticity of the elaborate speech of the Indian youths, he says after he had written the passage and after Silvestre had read and edited it, as was customary in their procedure, it occurred to him to question Silvestre about disbelief that the orations were sure to arouse, given the low opinion in which Indians were commonly held.

Silvestre's reply was completely reassuring. There was no need to give any thought to opinions of the ignorant except to nullify them by speaking the truth. There were Indians with good minds, capable of speaking effectively. Garcilaso quotes him as saying that the speeches represented in substance what the Indians had said, that there had been many other fine speeches which he could not remember, and that even if he could remember them, he could not report the exact words they used. The eloquence of the Indians had impressed de Soto, and some of the educated men of the company went so far as to say that those Indians seemed to have been educated in Athens at the height of her glory. He encouraged Garcilaso to write with all the exaggeration at his command; it would not be excessive. Silvestre concluded, "Therefore write without any scruple what I tell you, whether they believe it or not, for with having spoken the truth about what happened we fulfil our obligation, and to do otherwise would be an offense to those concerned."

The chapter ends with a final statement from Garcilaso: "All this, as I have said, happened to me with my author and I set it down here so that it may be understood and believed that we venture to write the truth rather with a lack of the elegance and rhetoric necessary to give the deeds their proper place than with excess of hyperbole because I am not capable of it and because in the future, in matters as great and greater that we will observe, it will be necessary to reinforce our reputation for credibility. I say no more now, but let us return to our history."

The chapter is interesting and significant because it is eloquent testimony to Garcilaso's constant preoccupation, in the *Florida,* in the *Comentarios reales* and in the *Historia general del Perú,* with writing what he considered to be the truth. He may seem to protest too much and his readers may well be astonished at his acceptance of Silvestre's reassurances in the matter. The point here is not that Garcilaso gave what could by any stretch of the imagination be considered an objectively accurate rendering of speeches he never heard, but that he believed he was giving the essence of what was said and even, perhaps, the essence of the style in which it was said. He defends here a specific technique that did at a later date provoke the criticism he foresaw, and along with it his whole method of writing history.

Garcilaso considers possible the criticism of a narrative based on the recollections of a participant in the action recorded; such recollections may give a distorted picture and may exaggerate the deeds of the narrator. It may be asked, he admits, how can one who fought in a battle have seen the whole battle and how can one who saw the battle as a whole have fought in it? Garcilaso has no difficulty countering such objections; it was the custom for the soldiers to report all items of interest to the captains and the general, apparently in public, and all events worthy of any note were verified immediately. Thus Silvestre was in a position to report not only his own activities but those of his companions. Garcilaso was of some assistance to Silvestre because by dint of questioning and requestioning, he helped him to recall happenings long past.

One of the greatest problems Garcilaso encountered in putting together his materials, which came to him in fragments, was to establish the chronology of the expedition and to confirm names of persons and places. In the case of the material he obtained from Silvestre, the difficulty of setting events in their correct order was particularly great; the long period of consultation in which he picked up bits and pieces of the narrative as Silvestre recalled his youth undoubtedly yielded vast quantities of notes that required extraordinary patience and close attention to detail in order to produce anything resembling a coherent narrative.

Neither Carmona nor Coles was concerned about chronology. From Garcilaso's description of their manuscripts, they were scarcely different in respect to organization from the conversation of Silvestre. Only at the beginning do they observe the proper relationship of events. As they moved on in their narratives, they put down what they remembered simply as it occurred to them, sometimes anticipating, sometimes postponing. They are particularly unsatisfactory in the matter of place names which they provide only occasionally.

The problems of geography plagued Garcilaso even more than problems of chronology. He was at a decided disadvantage since he himself had never even seen Florida and useful maps were nonexistent. He complains frequently in the history about the almost total unconcern of the explorers for distances and directions. His eyewitness sources were excellent for some things, but it is not surprising that they gave so little heed to exactly where they were and where they were going. None of the three was in fact in a position of responsibility; their attentions were absorbed by problems of survival and by the orders of their commanders.

Garcilaso is frustrated more than once because he is unable to give anything but the vaguest idea of the direction taken. At one point he feels it necessary to warn his reader, "This direction, and all others that are mentioned in this history, are not to be taken as exact, lest I be blamed if it should prove otherwise when that land is won, God be pleased, for although I made every effort necessary to be able to record them with certainty, I was unable to accomplish it. . . . This is enough to excuse me for not having written with the certainty that I have desired and which was necessary." (II,[1] 12) At the end of the book, he is faced with the problem of the distance the army sailed down the Mississippi to its mouth. Here he has such conflicting statements that he concludes it will not be known until the land is conquered. It was no small task to bring to light even the little information he can give since so much time has passed and the explorers were so little concerned about such matters. "Therefore I must be allowed here the excuse I have given elsewhere for the faults of this history in matters of cosmography; I should like to have written it very fully in order to give greater and better information about that land." (VI, 9)

VII   The Florida *as Narrative*

As one of the few contemporary and near-contemporary records of the exploration of Florida, Garcilaso's history would have a certain value no matter what its style and form. It is read today, both in Spanish and in translation, where the other accounts are ignored except by specialists. A large part of the appeal of the *Florida* is due to Garcilaso's elaboration upon the bare facts of the action by adding materials that, however doubtful they may be from the scientific, historical point of view, do give an added attraction to the work.

Garcilaso is a rambling writer who, though he always has his eye on the main line of his narrative, often wanders away from it to discuss peripheral matters suggested to him by some element in the story he is telling. Some of the added materials seem at first glance irrelevant, but for the most part they do have some bearing upon what Garcilaso is trying to accomplish. He never lost sight of his purpose any more than he did of the thread of his narrative. He wants to influence public opinion to favor the settlement and Christianization of Florida; for him the uses of history are didactic and moral.

As he proceeds in his report of the encounters between Spaniards and Indians, he often pauses to discuss the Indian culture. The first of these digressions occurs in Book I, Chapter 4, where he describes what he considers to be some of the customs generally followed by the Indians in the whole area crossed by the expedition. He briefly describes the religion, pointing out that, while they worshipped the sun and the moon, they used none of the idols, sacrifices, prayers or other superstitions common to other heathen people. Their temples were only tombs and were not used as places of worship. There is a short account of marriage customs, their diet, their clothing and adornments, their weapons. Because it was a sensitive point in connection with the Incan civilization, Garcilaso takes special pains to deny, wherever he can, the existence of cannibalism among the Indians. The Indians of Florida abhorred the practice; in fact, the only cannibalism in the area was that practised by the starving Spaniards of Narváez' expedition. He cites Alvar Núñez Cabeza de Vaca's *Naufragios* as support for the statement that the Indians were appalled by the Spaniards' actions. He protects himself against error by admitting that possibly, since Florida was so broad and long, cannibalism did exist in areas not touched by de Soto.

In the course of his history, he returns at times to elaborate upon customs or to account for local differences. In Book III, Chapter 12, he gives fuller information about the arrows used and the great esteem in which they were held. He devotes the whole of Chapter 34 of that book to a discussion of the stern laws against adultresses in the provinces of Coza and Tascaluza. Garcilaso was not without a sense of humor. Admitting that he knew nothing about laws against adulterers, and assuming that there were none, he adds, "It must be that way for these laws are always and in all nations stern against women and in favor of men, because, as a duenna of this bishopric whom I knew said, men made them being fearful of the offense, not the women, for if women had made them they would have been ordained in a different fashion."

Frequently he stops to give a description of the vegetation found along the march. Near the coast were many of the trees found in Spain, oak, walnut, mulberry, plum and pine, which gave the landscape a gentle, pleasant appearance. Farther to the north were great forests of pine and walnut along with many other trees unknown to the Spaniards. Fields of corn, beans and squash were found and the appearance of the maguey produces a discussion of its many uses.

Garcilaso does not give detailed descriptions of all the towns the expedition entered but he does so often enough to give an idea of the varied nature of the settlements. Mauvila, different from many of the others, consisted of some eight houses, but these houses were so large that the smallest of them sheltered five hundred people, the largest fifteen hundred. The whole town was surrounded by a wall in which defensive towers were set at intervals. Another kind of fortified town was found on the banks of the Mississippi. The principal feature here was a great moat. Sometimes only the most imposing building of a town is described, as in the case of the great temple found in the province of the Lady of Cofachiqui.

All variety of subjects is introduced into the narrative. A discussion of the names applied to the several racial mixtures found in the New World interrupts the story of de Soto's search for a passage through the great swamp. The Indian method of extracting pearls from the oyster shells offers material for another digression. To demonstrate that the Indians were in need of conversion and to show how easily they could be converted, Garcilaso gives the story of the Indian guide Pedro who, convinced he was possessed of the devil, was restored to health when he was baptized. Garcilaso points out that Pedro's account of what happened to him would have been enough to convert all the people of his province but unfortunately the members of the expedition were not concerned with missionary activity and did not take advantage of the opportunity offered.

Throughout the *Florida*, Garcilaso shows a marked tendency toward moralistic commentary on his subject matter. These commentaries are often in aphoristic style, inserted almost casually in the text. At the end of a paragraph extolling the noble qualities of Carlos Enríquez, slain in the battle at Mauvila, Garcilaso adds, "There can be no nobility where there is no virtue." (III, 30) Commenting upon the fine qualities of a young Indian noble, he reveals his aristocratic attitude with the remark, "Where there is nobility of blood there must be generosity of spirit for they go together like the fruit and the tree." (III, 11) The actions of two Indians surprised by a group of Spanish soldiers elicits the comment that "fortune favors the bold since they merit it"; the cowardly Indian who fled was slain, the more daring one was spared because the Spaniards admired his spirit. (II,[2] 9) Once Garcilaso denies the truth of a proverbial expression to emphasize Juan Ortiz' bravery in killing a lion, "although the proverb says lions are not as fierce as they are painted, those who have been close to them say live ones are much fiercer than painted ones." (II,[1] 3)

When the short, sententious line does not meet his needs, Garcilaso introduces a paragraph or two of comment upon the situation he has been considering. A recurring theme for these discourses is the use of power and wealth and their effects upon those who possess them. After he relates Vasco Porcallo de Figueroa's embarrassment resulting from an unfortunate attempt to capture an Indian chief and his decision to abandon the expedition, taking all his soldiers and slaves back to Cuba, Garcilaso analyzes the impulsive character of the ambitious general, the motives that lay behind his ill-considered action and his refusal to accept advice, the happier results that would have been achieved had he not been so confident of his own great talents. This overconfidence Garcilaso attributes to Vasco Porcallo's advantageous circumstances. "But who is there to tame a wild beast or to counsel the free and powerful, confident of themselves and persuaded that they have riches of the mind in the same proportion as they have material wealth, and that as they have advantage over other men in the wealth they have not earned, so they excel others in discretion and wisdom which they have not learned? Wherefore they neither seek counsel, nor do they wish to receive it, nor can they tolerate those who are willing to give it." (II,¹ 12)

Nuño Tovar's situation presented a case quite different from Vasco Porcallo's. Tovar, though in de Soto's disfavor because of his clandestine marriage with de Soto's ward, remained a loyal follower of the commander and distinguished himself by gallant, generous actions. He bore with equanimity de Soto's scorn and never let his noble spirit be betrayed into unworthy actions. Princes and powerful men who are tyrants rarely or never are reconciled with those who have offended them, rather their feeling of offense increases when the offender acts virtuously. Garcilaso surely speaks from the heart when he concludes, "Therefore, in my poor opinion, let the one who finds himself in such a position go beg for his food, if he does not have it, rather than persist in such service because whatever miracles he may perform, they will not suffice to restore him to favor." (II,¹ 14) It will be recalled that the *Diálogos de amor* were dedicated to the King; it was the last time Garcilaso made that dedication.

The refusal of Mucozo, the benefactor of Juan Ortiz, to return the Spaniard to his captor on the grounds that honor demanded that he protect the life of one placed in his care, aroused Garcilaso's admiration. He compares Mucozo's generous action to the behavior of Christian princes who have taken hostages from pagan nations and have betrayed their trust. Those Christians "breaking the laws of their kingdoms, without respecting their own being and rank, for they were kings and great princes, scorning their promised, sworn faith, a thing unworthy of such names, only to relieve their anger exchanged those who had not offended them for those who had, exchanging the innocent for the guilty as ancient and modern histories bear witness. Which matters we will now leave in order not to offend powerful ears and distress the pious." (II,¹ 4) It would be most interesting to know to what specific events Garcilaso refers here and whose powerful ears he risked offending. One suspects that the betrayal of the innocent refers in some way to the Indians of Peru and that the faithless leader was conceivably the King of Spain.

It is generally agreed among historians that the *Florida* is basically a true account of the adventures and misadventures of de Soto and his men. The reader who may be tempted to accept all the work at face value as a record of the expedition is warned to read with some skepticism; Garcilaso has been suspected as an historian because of a well-marked tendency toward romance which transforms the reality he is reporting and lends his history an air of fantasy. Although Garcilaso presents himself modestly as being only the scribe for Silvestre, the final product is as much Garcilaso's as it is Silvestre's. Some of the quality of romance may very well be attributed to the accounts Garcilaso had from his principal sources, three old soldiers remembering and embroidering past experiences, distorting and exaggerating personal triumphs and hardships, but fundamentally the creation of mood and atmosphere is the work of Garcilaso. He denied interest in novels of chivalry but, like many of his contemporaries, he was unable to avoid their pervasive influence.

Many of the episodes and incidents in the work, as Aurelio Miró Quesada has pointed out, owe much to the Spanish romances of chivalry, the Renaissance epics of Ariosto and Boiardo, and the Byzantine novel.[5] The courtly manners of the Indians, the chivalric code of honor observed by some of the Indian chiefs, the introduction of the sentimental love story of Diego Guzmán who left the expedition to follow a fair Indian maiden, the unexpected encounters, the violent storms, the shipwrecks and the happy reconciliations, all bear more resemblance to fiction than to historical fact. These elements alone do not give the *Florida* its lasting appeal; other aspects of Garcilaso's literary genius contribute even more to the memorable account of de Soto's expedition.

As a work of literary art, the *Florida* is by far the most satisfactory of Garcilaso's work, perhaps because it does have so many of the qualities of the novel. The work is organized with a beginning, middle and end. Book I serves as introduction, Books II through V contain the heart of the narrative, Book VI stands as summary which relates the fates of the surviving members of the company. It is in the middle section that Garcilaso reveals his skill as a writer of narrative. The story is not composed merely of a succession of events with no other logical relationship than their having occurred during the course of the expedition. Like a novel, the history is built of a series of major episodes, each containing a wealth of incident, anecdote, description, and commentary, all related one to the other through the major unit.

The organization of Book III offers an excellent example of Garcilaso's basic method. The first nine chapters are concerned with the march from Apalache to Cofachiqui; ten chapters contain the events relating to the Lady of Cofachiqui; four chapters are devoted to the march from Cofachiqui to Mauvila; twelve contain the story of the fearful Tascaluza and the battle at Mauvila; the last four are an account of the battle of Chicaza. This is the arrangement followed in the whole history, a series of major episodes—in which progress in space is not important—linked together by passages whose purpose is to carry the narrative forward in time and space. Garcilaso dwells on the episodes involving the Lady of Cofachiqui and Tascaluza because they reveal far more of the Indian culture and the Spanish reactions to it than do the reports of movement from place to place.

Garcilaso shows great versatility in his method of presentation of these major episodes, alternating general summary with more complete and detailed accounts of specific events. The story is revealed not through a consistent point of view but with constantly shifting focus. At times the point of view is that of an objective observer, Garcilaso himself, who has effectively erased his sources so far as their discernible presence is concerned, who relates what has happened but who reveals nothing of what is in the minds of the characters. Often Garcilaso intrudes in his own person to comment subjectively upon the action. Again the narrator is the omniscient or analytic author who presents the working of the mind of the character, who investigates and interprets motives and feelings. Sometimes the point of view is plainly that of an observer who is also a participant in the action, the soldiers Silvestre, Carmona, and Coles.

Garcilaso's effective handling of his materials greatly enhances the interest of the narrative. An event that might otherwise pass almost unnoticed, or at best be given cursory attention, often is transformed in his hands into an intense, dramatic moment. Of the twenty-five chapters that compose the second part of Book II, seven are devoted to the story of thirty soldiers sent under the command of Juan de Añasco to recall Pedro Calderón and his group to the general's camp. The trip was a difficult and perilous one, the Indians were unfriendly, and the terrain offered a constant challenge to the endurance of the Spaniards. At one point, the group, broken up while crossing a flooded river on a raft, is attacked. In itself the incident is an exciting one, but of no particular consequence either to the history of the expedition as a whole or to the story of the march of the thirty. Garcilaso builds a vivid and suspenseful scene by starting with a brief general description of the activity, including the building of the raft, and of the natural setting in which it occurred, and then, by progressively reducing the number of men upon whom attention is focused. The whole company is involved in the preparations for crossing the river; when the Indians suddenly attack, it is eleven men who meet it. On the opposite side of the river, four soldiers are left to fight off the attack there. Finally only two men are left. The effect of this technique of constant reduction is to sharpen the dramatic effect of the narrative.

Like the omniscient novelist, Garcilaso reveals the internal states of his characters. After the treacherous Vitachuco plots the destruction of the Spaniards with their interpreters, Garcilaso tells his reader: "With great inner contentment, the proud Vitachuco and the four Indian interpreters broke up their consultation." There follows a description of Vitachuco's dreams of glory in which he sees himself honored as the liberator of the region, he hears the shouts of praise and even "imagined the songs which the women and children, dancing in a ring before him, would sing." (II,[1] 23) Vasco Porcallo emerges from his attempt to capture the Indian chief covered with mud and humiliated. To deal with his state of mind, Garcilaso approaches the interior monologue: "And, as to the anger at this misfortune was added the memory of his great wealth and the ease and comfort he had left at home and that he was no longer young and that the greater part of his life was already past and that the future labors of that conquest, all, or most, would be like those of that day, or worse, and that he had no need to assume them of his own will, for the ones he had already endured were enough for him, it seemed to him that he should leave that expedition to the young men. With these thoughts he went along the road, speaking sometimes to himself, sometimes aloud." (II,[1] 11)

Although Garcilaso showed some concern about the acceptability of the eloquent orations delivered by his Indians, many sections of the *Florida* are rendered by a method that today belongs to the novelist and dramatist rather than to the historian. Garcilaso never hesitates to supply speech for his characters; few chapters in the book fail to record words spoken either in public or in private. Since Garcilaso did have the testimony of eyewitnesses, it would have been satisfactory from the historian's point of view if he had given summaries of speeches remembered by those who were present. Garcilaso is rarely content with so flat a method. He is more inclined to sacrifice historical accuracy in favor of a scene developed entirely through dialogue, in direct or indirect quotation. However slight the justification for these scenes as history, they are good narrative; they add animation and allow the reader a closer view of the how and why of developments.

Garcilaso's re-creation of the emotional tone aids greatly in bringing to life many of the events and in giving a vitality to the characters. He encourages the direct participation of the reader with nothing more than "It aroused compassion and pity to see how the Spaniards emerged from the water . . ." (II,[2] 15) or with the parenthetical remark "for anyone can imagine how it must have been." (II,[2] 14) There are descriptions of externally observable emotional reactions of his characters, usually accompanied by some physical action, as when he relates the visit of Mucozo's mother to the Spanish camp: "With these words the good old woman became somewhat calmer, and stayed with the Spaniards three days, but always so shy and suspicious, that eating at the governor's table, she asked Juan Ortiz whether she dared eat what they gave her; she said she feared and suspected that they would give her poison to kill her." (II,[1] 8)

The value of character analysis and portrayal in a history was not lost on Garcilaso; hardly a personage of any consequence is presented without some description of his character. Usually Garcilaso depends upon the words and deeds of the individual to give some insight into his nature. The sterling qualities of Mucozo are revealed when he saves Juan Ortiz from the wrath of his captor and when he addresses a noble speech to de Soto. The reaction of the Spaniards to his words intensifies the favorable impression.

No Indian encountered by the Spaniards was more impressive than the Lady of Cofachiqui, a paragon of physical, moral, and intellectual beauty. Her magnificence is revealed gradually, the first hint of it coming from her ambassadors who announce themselves as the vassals of a marriageable young woman who had only recently come into her inheritance. The lady and her court are soon seen approaching in canoes; a suggestion of her regality is provided by a comparison with Cleopatra's coming out to greet Marc Anthony. The anticipation is not disappointed; when she speaks she reveals her true dignity and generosity. The reader fully shares the reaction of the Spaniards who were amazed to hear such fine, well-ordered words from a barbarian born and brought up without the benefits of civilization. She knew well enough how to hold her audience with something besides words. All during the time she was speaking, she was slowly removing a necklace of pearls large as filberts, so long that it made three turns about her neck and descended to her hips; with her concluding words she handed the necklace to Juan Ortiz with instructions to present it to de Soto. It is a small wonder that the Spaniards were so entranced with her that "neither then nor later did they try to find out what her name was, but contented themselves with calling her Lady and they were right, because she was one in all ways." (III, 11)

The *Florida* is the story of a group action in which all varieties of character are seen, from the noblest to the basest. The whole history, however, really depends upon the character of one man whose moral collapse assured the failure of the expedition. Garcilaso reveals the focus of his narrative with his opening words, "The Adelantado Hernando de Soto . . . whose story this is, along with that of many other Spanish and Indian knights . . ." At no point does Garcilaso offer a complete analysis of de Soto; he sustains interest in the character by centering attention on him from time to time throughout the work. The man is revealed gradually; it is only after his death that the reader has a comprehensive idea of him.

Brief summaries dwell on aspects of de Soto's character in the introduction, at the moment of his collapse, and after his death. After a discussion of the weakness that led to de Soto's downfall, in which he points out the wisdom of taking the advice of his trustworthy friends, Garcilaso concludes, "This captain could have prevented that insurrection by punishing its leaders, from which the rest of the league, who were few, would have taken warning, and he would not have ruined himself and damaged his own people by governing only by his impassioned opinion which caused his own destruction. For, although he was, as we have seen, so discerning in his own affairs, but being angered he could not govern himself with the clarity and free judgment that serious matters require. Therefore let him who avoids seeking and taking counsel give up hope of succeeding." (III, 33) Most commonly Garcilaso presents de Soto in action—his conduct in the face of danger, his relations with the army and with the Indians—and leaves the reader to draw his own conclusions.

The death of de Soto offers an opportunity for showing the reaction of the men to the personality of their leader: "The death of the governor and captain general Hernando de Soto, so worthy of being mourned, caused great grief and sadness in all his men, as much because of having lost him and because of their being left orphans—for they considered him a father—as because of not being able to give him the burial his body deserved nor to offer the solemn obsequies they would have liked to offer so beloved a captain and lord." (V,[1] 8) When de Soto learns of the planned rebellion, Garcilaso gives a glimpse into his mind: "The governor regretted this exceedingly because he understood from those words that his army was breaking up and that his men, as soon as they found a place to go, were all leaving him . . . and that he had no possibility of forming a new army and that he was stripped of his greatness, authority and reputation, his wealth squandered and the excessive labor that he had endured up to that point in the discovery of that land wasted." (III, 33)

In his treatment of time, Garcilaso shows a great advance over the rigorously chronological methods of the earlier chroniclers. For all his admiration of order in time, he finds it appropriate to depart from it and constantly disarranges the basic chronological order, thereby creating highly desirable variations in his narrative. He sometimes finds it advisable to relate a previously reported event to a subsequent one; this is accomplished by backward glances introduced by such tags as "as we have seen before," "as we mentioned before," "earlier we told how." In such cases, the first event, repeated after having been reported in its proper place, serves to bring past and present together for a fuller understanding of the present. In similar fashion, the interest of the reader is teased and suspense is aroused by the brief looks forward in which future events are hinted at: "Tascaluza was a proud and warlike man, with many tricks and much cunning as we will see later." (III, 23)

Occasionally Garcilaso says that he has forgotten to report an item that belonged chronologically to another part of his story. The first impression is that of a naive and unskilled narrator: "We forgot to tell earlier in its place about an exemplary punishment which Captain Patofa gave one of his Indians. Because it is so unusual, it should not be forgotten, and will fit in wherever it is placed." (III, 7) It is highly doubtful that Garcilaso placed the incident where he did simply because he had forgotten about it. Patofa is a prominent figure in the chapter; the story of the Indian's punishment reveals something of the character of the Spaniard and is most appropriate in the place it occupies.

Since there were times when he had nothing of particular interest to report, Garcilaso may resort to a telescoping technique, skimming over periods of time that are often lengthy: "In all the time the Spaniards were wintering in Utiangue, which was more than five months, nothing of moment except what has been told took place." (V,[1] 1) The matters of moment he mentions consist largely of receiving an occasional Indian visitor and of hunting for their food.

It is not uncommon to find exactly the opposite of telescoping of time in the *Florida*. In Chapter 21 of Book III there is little interesting action to report. The main body of the expedition is encamped, awaiting the return of two soldiers who had gone off to investigate a report of gold mines. Garcilaso fills the chapter with an account of the Indian method of fishing for pearls, of the finding of a particularly large one, and with the story of an accidental death in the camp. He says that he has included the section on pearls to show the richness of the land. There is no such reason for including the accidental death. At the beginning of the next chapter, the expedition sets out again upon the return of the two explorers. The inconsequential details of Chapter 21, in spite of what the author says, are really unimportant to history, but they do have a definite artistic purpose: they slow down the narrative, fill in while the pair sent in search of gold goes and returns, heightening the illusion of the idleness of the army.

It was not Garcilaso's intention to write a novel; he was concerned with history, but history with a purpose. He was in effect writing propaganda. His basic material was factual; the events he had to describe occurred in definite order and place, the persons who took part in the action were real, the outcome of the conflict was known. In re-creating the world in which de Soto and his men operated, Garcilaso felt the need to heighten the illusion of reality, an effect accomplished by the logical organization, the emphasizing (or minimizing) of events, the changes in method for dealing with character delineation and chronology, the shifting point of view, and the emotional evocation of the mood of particular moments. The air and interest of a novel come to Garcilaso's history only in part from his conscious or unconscious borrowings from the conventions of romance; the success of the *Florida* as narrative depends even more on the author's skillful use of varied techniques to present his story.

CHAPTER 5

The Comentarios reales

IN Lisbon in 1609, Pedro Crasbeeck published the book that brought Garcilaso his greatest success and the one that established him as one of the historians of the Incan empire who must be taken into account by any later writers on the subject. This second book of Garcilaso was dedicated to Doña Catalina de Portugal, Duquesa de Braganza, under the explanatory title: *Primera parte de los Comentarios Reales, que tratan del origen de los Yncas, reyes que fueron del Peru, de su idolatria, leyes, y govierno en paz y en guerra: de sus vidas y conquistas, y de todo lo que fue aquel imperio y su republica, antes que los españoles passaran a el. Escritos por el Ynca Garcilaso de la Vega, natural del Cozco y capitan de su Majestad* (First Part of the Royal Commentaries, which deal with the origin of the Incas, former kings of Peru, with their idolatry, laws, and government in peace and in war: with their lives and conquests and with everything concerning that empire and its public affairs before the coming of the Spaniards. Written by the Inca Garcilaso de la Vega, native of Cuzco and His Majesty's captain).

I *Résumé*

The first of the nine books of the *Comentarios* opens with a geographical discussion, aimed mainly at establishing the fact that although Peru is in the Torrid Zone it is habitable. Garcilaso reviews the history of the discovery of America with particular attention to the story of Alonso Sánchez de Huelva who, according to Garcilaso, reached the New World before Columbus. He gives the theories concerning the origin of the name Peru and adds information on other place-names imposed by the Spaniards. Chapter 8 begins with a description of the limits of the empire at the arrival of the Spaniards, but Garcilaso soon drops that matter to tell the story of the shipwrecked Pedro Serrano ". . . so that this chapter will not be so short." With Chapter 9 he begins to deal with his real material, the establishment of the Inca dynasty. The natives of the Andean region before the coming of Manco Capac were living in a state of unbearable barbarism, particularly in matters of religion. They worshipped the things they could see, emeralds, wild animals, and plants. While marriage customs varied, nowhere did they approach the civilized. Chaotic conditions were not helped by the great number of languages spoken. Garcilaso makes some attempt to distinguish practices according to locality, particularly in the question of human sacrifices and of cannibalism, the existence of which proves for Garcilaso the need of divine aid. In the matter of clothing, or rather the lack of it, Garcilaso displays a prudish attitude; he is happier about the Indians in the cold regions who were forced to cover themselves with animal skins as protection from the climate.

According to tradition, the sun took pity upon these heathen and sent his son and daughter to bring them out of the shadows into the light. They were set down at Lake Titicaca with a golden bar. Wherever the bar sank into the earth, they were to establish their Court. The first Inca, Manco Capac, and his sister-wife were to convert and teach the heathen; as a reward they were constituted kings and lords of all the people they could persuade to join them. Cuzco proved to be the chosen spot; there the Incan empire was established. Manco Capac immediately began the task of expanding his influence, always to the benefit of the barbarians. Garcilaso gives other legends concerning the arrival of the first Inca. He closes the book with an account of Manco Capac's will and his death and a discussion of the names and titles given to the royal family.

Book II returns to the question of religion, the establishment of the worship of the sun, with the kings worshipped as descendants of the sun. This, for Garcilaso, was an obvious advance over the pre-Inca religion with its multiplicity of gods. He maintains that the Incas were working toward a concept of the Christian God with their worship of a spirit, Pachacamac, who, being the creator of all things, was held in even greater veneration than the sun. One of the serious errors of Spanish historians, according to Garcilaso, was the attribution of a great number of gods to the Incas; the error stems, he says, from a misinterpretation of the word *huaca* which did not always mean divinity. The Incas had developed a belief in the immortality of the soul and in universal resurrection. The methods and materials of sacrifice are described with another denial of the practice of human sacrifice by the Incas. The first Inca founded a priesthood and established laws governing it.

The territory conquered by Manco Capac was divided into four parts, with Cuzco at their center. In each of these parts the population was organized by decuries. The smallest division was of ten individuals, one of whom was leader; five leaders of these small groups chose one of their number to lead the fifty. This method expanded so that there were decuries of ten, fifty, a hundred, five hundred and a thousand. The decurion of each group was responsible for those under his charge and to the leader of the next larger unit. They were charged with maintaining law and order, but had the further duty of keeping census records.

The reign of the second Inca, Sinchi Roca, offered comparatively little to record except for some expansion of the Inca influence over neighboring tribes. His successor was Lloque Yupanqui who gathered an army of six or seven thousand men to bring into the fold certain neighboring groups who had not yielded to peaceful persuasion. The sight of the army was evidently enough for some groups; others required sterner measures. One group misunderstood the Inca's gentle methods of warfare, siege rather than open battle, and grew bold enough to attack even the Inca's headquarters. A battle followed; the defeated barbarians returned to their fortress where they were finally starved into submission. The Inca's generosity toward them convinced others in the vicinity that it would be well to ally themselves with Tahuantinsuyu, as the Incan empire was called. After a number of years, the Inca made a tour of all his territories, and followed it with another military campaign. With Lloque Yupanqui the pattern for succeeding reigns is set: conquest, a period of consolidation including an inspection tour, further conquests in which the heir often participates, a deathbed speech naming the successor and reminding him of his duties as outlined by Manco Capac. Eight chapters at the end of the book are devoted to Incan accomplishments in astronomy, medicine, geometry, geography, arithmetic, music, philosophy, poetry, and the mechanical arts.

Book III opens with the beginning of the reign of Mayta Capac, who carried on the missionary work begun by his predecessors with an army of twelve thousand. Most of the provinces yielded gracefully, having had advance notice of the superiority of the Incan civilization and of the favored treatment received by those who offered no resistance. With those who did resist, the Inca displayed his customary generosity. After a period of rest and consolidation, Mayta Capac set out on another successful campaign during which Incan engineering genius so impressed the people of several towns that they immediately recognized the value of joining the Inca. It was the construction of a wicker bridge, described in considerable detail, that accomplished the Inca's purpose. After his return to Cuzco, Mayta Capac dismissed his army and devoted the rest of his life to the good government of his kingdom, paying particular heed to the needs of the poor, widows and orphans.

He was succeeded by his son, Capac Yupanqui, who continued to extend the area of Incan influence in much the same way his father had done. He did introduce a different method for attracting new provinces to his protection. He agreed to act as arbitrator in a particularly vicious quarrel between two chiefs. After the Inca listened to all the evidence, he informed the two that his father, the sun, decreed that they should observe the laws of the Incas, give up their senseless warfare, and concern themselves with the welfare of their people. The advice was so sensible that the chiefs decided to accept it, influenced only in part by the fact that Capac Yupanqui's conquests were bringing him very close to their borders and that they would soon have to accept domination by the Inca.

After the usual account of the death of the Inca, Garcilaso devotes several chapters to a description of the great Temples of the Sun in Cuzco and at Titicaca with all their rich adornment.

More than half of Book IV is devoted to the life of women in the Incan empire, beginning with an account of the House of the Virgins in Cuzco. Garcilaso says that since Spanish historians treat the subject gingerly, it would be well for him to explain exactly what was involved in the system. As he describes it, the House of the Virgins was similar in some respects to Catholic convents, in other respects to the Temple of the Vestal Virgins in Rome. They were all of pure royal blood, since they were considered wives of the sun. Their principal duty was to weave cloth for the clothing of the Inca and his queen, as well as the garments that were offered as sacrifice to the sun.

Marriage ceremonies, both of the common people and of royalty, the laws of inheritance, the weaning and naming of infants, the domestic duties of women are all discussed before the reign of the sixth Inca, Inca Roca, is mentioned.

Inca Roca began his reign in the usual fashion, though he was supported by an increased army of twenty thousand which grew

to thirty thousand during his last campaign. Faithful to his duty of
adding territory, he made an even greater contribution by opening
state schools for the nobles. Yahuar Huacac, whose name means
"he who weeps blood," was the next in succession. He had made
a successful military campaign while still crown prince, but when
he became king he was seized with doubt because of the supersti-
tious association with his name; as a result, he hesitated to lead his
armies personally. Finally forced by public opinion, he took the field
and acquired the usual additions of territory. His problems were
not ended, however; his son was so recalcitrant that it became necessary to banish him. After three years, the prince appeared, in defi-
ance of his father's orders, to report a vision in which the spirit
Viracocha, brother of Manco Capac, had told him to warn the Inca
of rebellion within the empire. Yahuar Huacac was angered and
sent his son back to his place of exile, but three months later the
rebellion did break out. The Inca, disliking war to the point of
cowardice, fled the capital. The prince, distressed by his father's
lack of valor, raised an army and set out to restore order in the
empire.

In Book V, the story of Yahuar Huacac is suspended while Garcilaso discourses upon matters relating to agriculture, the supply of
food for the empire, methods of land distribution and the collection
of tributes. One of the first considerations after the conquest of a
territory was to improve its agricultural methods by constructing
terraces and irrigation canals so that every bit of land possible could
be made tillable and as highly productive as possible. The land was
divided into three parts; one for the sun, one for the Inca, and one
for the vassals. This last third was to supply the needs of each village;
if the village lands were not sufficient to provide the necessary food,
they were augmented from the fields dedicated to the sun and the
Inca. The fields of the sun were those first cultivated, the Inca's, last.
A system of granaries was established to assure a supply of food
for all throughout the year. Gold, silver and precious stones had no
meaning except as things of natural beauty; they were therefore
presented to the Incas as gifts, not as taxes. The tribute demanded
was labor in the production of food for the poor, clothing and
weapons for the army, extra supplies of which were kept in storehouses throughout the empire.

Halfway through the book Garcilaso returns to the story of the
prince, known as Viracocha, who was determined to protect the
capital. He met the enemy outside the city and after a fierce battle

emerged victorious. His early delinquency cast aside, Viracocha behaved in traditional Inca fashion by treating the defeated rebels with kindness. He disbanded his army and reported to his father who, in order to avoid civil war, abdicated and retired to the country. Garcilaso reports that the legend of the prince's vision was of supreme importance to the Spaniards since the appearance of the spirit Viracocha, as described by his namesake, was very like that of the Spaniards. They were thus in an advantageous position from the very beginning, being considered as emissaries from God to free the Incas from the tyranny of Atahualpa. Viracocha enjoyed great prestige because of the divine favor shown him and because of his own wisdom and bravery which contrasted so sharply with the qualities of his father. To celebrate his great achievements, he built a magnificent temple dedicated to his guardian spirit; he distinguished his reign by devoting great attention to lawmaking and the construction of public buildings.

Like the others, Book VI is a combination of materials; here however, the events of the reign of the Inca Pachacutec are given in two parts, each preceded by a section on civilization. The royal palaces with their opulent decorations of gold and silver put to shame all other palaces in the world. The sacred rooms and those used by the Inca were lined with gold, human and animal figures of gold were placed in all the rooms; even the gardens were filled with gold and silver animals, all appropriately and naturally placed among the plants. The servants necessary to maintain the royal establishments were furnished by certain villages, honored with the privilege of supplying the necessary royal attendants. Garcilaso devotes a chapter to royal funeral ceremonies and another to the custom of the royal hunt before he turns to the system of the *chasqui*, or the relay runners who carried official messages to all parts of the empire. Their messages were delivered either orally or by means of the elaborate system of knotted cords, the *quipu*, used to keep statistical records of all kinds. Other matters touched upon in the book are the ceremonies of the Festival of the Sun, the training of novice knights, reminiscent of medieval European customs, the ceremonial clothing of the knights and the special devices worn by the Incas.

The Inca Pachacutec delayed six years before he embarked upon the traditional duty of expanding his inherited territories, a duty which he pursued with great success, due in large part to the aid of his son and his brother. The conquests were pushed beyond

Cajamarca, where later Atahualpa became the prisoner of Pizarro. Pachacutec seems to have been the first of the Incas to entrust most of the military campaigns to his royal relatives. Pachacutec was one of the great Incas, not only because of the extensive conquests during his reign, but even more so because of his program of public construction, his reforms of laws, religious ceremony, and the militia, his expansion of the state schools, and his establishment of a single language to serve the whole empire. In the last chapter Garcilaso includes a list of Pachacutec's moral sentences which he found in Valera's biography of the Inca.

Book VII contains first an account of the Inca method of colonization designed both to prevent rebellion and to improve the living conditions of the people. Families were transferred from already established provinces to the new ones and some of the newly conquered would replace them in the more settled areas. Further to insure proper attitudes in the provinces, the Incas required that the heirs of all local chiefs be reared in Cuzco where they could be educated according to Incan precepts.

Two solemn festivals, the first intended to protect the newly-sprouted plants from frost, and the second to purge the city of evil spirits and diseases, complete Garcilaso's account of Incan ceremonies. A description of Cuzco fills five chapters with an additional three chapters at the end of the book devoted to the great fortress of the city.

The history of the empire is resumed with the accomplishments of the Inca Yupanqui which were modest compared with those of his father. He was not deterred by an unsuccessful campaign against the Chirihuanas, but laid plans for a great assault on the kingdom of Chile. Two armies of ten thousand each were sent out; they were able to gain some new territory, but finally met such fierce resistance from the barbarians that they decided to content themselves with what they had already won. Here Garcilaso inserts the history of Spanish attempts to conquer northern Chile, an undertaking that caused the Spaniards as much difficulty as it did the Incas.

The first chapters of Book VIII deal with the career of Tupac Inca Yupanqui who continued to push out the boundaries of the empire, constructing roads and bridges as he progressed and instructing his new vassals in the laws of the Incas. His progress was toward the north over difficult terrain and brought him to the borders of the kingdom of Quito. This rich and powerful kingdom was tempting, but its conquest was not easy. Tupac Inca Yupanqui soon discovered that his gracious offers, backed by an army of forty thousand, to make the kingdom a part of Tahuantinsuyu were not so graciously received. He placed his son Huaina Capac in supreme command and himself returned to Cuzco leaving the youthful prince to carry on the long war. He brought it to a successful conclusion and returned to Cuzco in triumph. Huaina Capac was unusual among the Incas in that he had three legitimate wives; his first marriage had produced no heir, so he was married to his second sister, the mother of Huascar, and his niece who became the mother of Manco Inca.

Since his history was approaching the time when the Spaniards appeared in Peru, Garcilaso felt it appropriate to give an account of the foodstuffs available before the introduction of European products. When he discusses the grains used, corn, quinoa, beans, he adds descriptions of the methods of preparing them. Root crops, fruits of all kinds, are listed and a chapter on the maguey and its uses is included. The uses of coca are given in detail. He lists the wild and domestic animals and birds, with a special chapter on parrots, and the fish that were useful to the native population. When he comes to the mineral wealth of the empire, Garcilaso lists emeralds, pearls, turquoises, gold, silver and mercury. It is interesting to note that he believes the emeralds undergo a ripening process like fruit and that the side of the stone exposed to the east ripens first.

Book IX continues the story of Huaina Capac. On the occasion of the birth of his son Huascar, he had a great golden chain made which the Indians were to carry in their ceremonial dances. So heavy that two hundred men could hardly carry it, the chain was greatly treasured by the Incas and was one of the pieces they hid from the Spaniards so successfully that it was never found. Huaina Capac, after his tour of the empire, returned to Quito where he spent considerable time embellishing the city with magnificent new buildings. It was during this period that he fathered Atahualpa and two other sons. He continued his warfare, adding still more to the empire. The people of the island of Puna betrayed Huaina Capac into one of the few ungenerous acts recorded by Garcilaso. When a large group of his captains and ministers were returning to the mainland on rafts, the resentful inhabitants of the island cut the ropes holding the rafts together and drowned the whole group. The Inca was so enraged at the loss of so many valued advisers that he could not forgive the guilty and ordered a massacre of thousands.

Before his death Huaina Capac obtained the agreement of his heir, Huascar, that Atahualpa should be given the kingdom of Quito and adjacent provinces. Huaina Capac left Cuzco in the hands of Huascar and returned with Atahualpa to Quito where he spent the remainder of his life. Shortly before his death, reports of strangers off the coast were brought to him; he was reminded of the ancient prediction that strangers would one day appear to destroy the Incan empire and religion. On his deathbed, Huaina Capac predicted that he would prove to be the last Inca, that the old prophecy would soon be realized. He ordered his people to obey their conquerors for their law would be superior to Inca law.

After a period of four or five years of peace in the empire, Huascar began to regret having lost the northern kingdoms and to fear possible trouble from Atahualpa. He asked that Atahualpa acknowledge himself Huascar's vassal. Atahualpa agreed, but secretly planned to overthrow his half-brother. This he accomplished; he took Huascar prisoner and attempted to destroy all the royal family who could have any conceivable claim to the throne. He was not successful; many escaped. In his last chapter, Garcilaso gives a list of those who survived the massacre.

II *Evolution of the* Comentarios

Like his other books, the *Comentarios* was a long time in the writing. Garcilaso never confides when and how the idea of writing the history of the Incan empire first occurred to him. In the dedication of the *Diálogos de amor*, dated January 19, 1586, he tells the King that after he has finished the *Florida* he intends to pass on to a work on the customs, rites, ceremonies and antiquities of Peru, but he gives no clue to the status of the book at that moment. The sketchy description makes no mention either of the political and military history or of the biographies of the Incas which form an integral part of the finished *Comentarios*. This may mean that in 1586 the project was still in large part an idea and had not reached anything approaching its final form. In the undated proem to the *Florida* he announces that he is in the process of composing and polishing the history of Peru. Here his description of the contents is very similar to the list that appears on the title page; he will deal with the origin of the Inca kings, their ancient customs, idolatry and conquests, their laws and the order of their government in peace and in war. In the text of the *Comentarios* he says he was working on Chapter 26 of Book II in 1602, and on Chapter 25 of Book VII in 1603. Whether in these years he was writing the first draft or was revising is not clear. One other date is mentioned in the text; in the last chapter of Book IX, he says that at the end of March, 1604, he is still awaiting a report on the outcome of a petition presented to the King by a group of descendants of the royal Incas.

Garcilaso must have considered the book completed, or nearly so, at the end of 1604, when he began to make arrangements for the license to publish. The approval was granted in Lisbon, November 26, 1604, and was signed by Luis dos Anjos who, in the usual form of these documents, says he has seen the *Comentarios*. He describes the contents, using the information given in the title, with the further note that there are seven books. Since the work, as it was finally published, contained nine books, Garcilaso must have made changes between 1604 and 1609. At least two possibilities suggest themselves. The original plan may have been to divide the whole work (which finally consisted of the *Comentarios* and the *Historia general del Perú*) into three parts rather than the two of its final version. The theoretical second book would likely have taken the history from the death of the Inca Yupanqui (end of Book VII) to the arrival of the Spaniards, with a theoretical third book to contain the history of the conquest and the establishment of the Spanish colony. The thought that the original plan was to divide the whole history into three parts is supported by a statement in the foreword, "Two other books are being written about the events that took place among the Spaniards in my country up to the year 1560, when I left it." One other possibility is that Garcilaso may have completed the account of the Inca rulers by the end of Book VII, but later added enough material to fill out the nine books that were finally published. There is some evidence that Garcilaso's plan was in a state of flux up to the moment it reached the hands of the printer. The last sentence of Book IX of the *Comentarios* ends, ". . . and with this we will enter the tenth book to deal with the heroic and incredible deeds of the Spaniards who won that empire." This tenth book became the second part of the *Comentarios,* or the *Historia general del Perú.*

III *Purpose of the* Comentarios

If there were but a single motive in Garcilaso's writing his history of the Incan civilization, it would be that of satisfaction of personal pride, derived from demonstrating to Spain what a truly magnificent heritage he and others like him had. There is no doubt that he was acutely conscious of his royal blood and that he never hesitated to draw attention to the fact. Other considerations also influenced him in writing what became a great hymn of praise for the glories of an empire destroyed by the Spaniards. In his Foreword he comments upon the brevity with which most Spanish historians of Peru have treated its history, upon the errors they have introduced because of their lack of knowledge of the Indian language. His love of country forced him into the task of presenting a clear, true account of affairs in Peru before the conquest. He is properly modest about his work, which was done only in the interests of truth. He protests that his sole purpose is to serve the Christian republic, to give thanks for the pagans' having been brought out of their idolatry into Christianity.

In fact, Garcilaso did much more than he says he intended; a considerable share of the *Comentarios* is devoted to accounts of the Indian culture with no reference to other histories. He produced, finally, not a series of comments and explanations, but a complete history of the empire. Yet the statements in the Foreword recur again and again in the *Comentarios* as if Garcilaso constantly felt pressed to justify and explain his forwardness in differing with established Spanish historians. In part, it has been this apologetic, diffident manner, observable in his other works as well, that has led to the conclusion that Garcilaso was rebuffed in Spain because of his mixed blood.

His choice of title is a curious one and in itself reveals something of Garcilaso's personality. He preferred not to label his work a history or a chronicle, terms that perhaps seemed too pretentious for his modest undertaking. Commentary on the work of others, in the interest of establishing truth, was as far as a humble Indian of little or no education should go. But if his nine books and 262 chapters are only commentary, the addition of the proud word "royal" as a qualifier poses something of a paradox. As the title stands, it is ambiguous. It may mean commentaries on royal affairs, but Garcilaso does not so limit himself; in the Foreword he promises to tell everything that can be told about the Indians, from the lowliest of the vassals to the kings. The title could also mean that the commentaries are royal by virtue of their author.

IV *Sources*

Garcilaso claimed a particularly favored position for writing the history of Tahuantinsuyu, as the Incan empire was called. He himself spoke the Indian language and was so able to interpret accurately accounts related by the Indians. He was able to question his informants to bring out information that would otherwise have been lost. In his childhood he absorbed much of the Indian tradition and philosophy. He could not have written the *Comentarios* only on the basis of what he remembered from his childhood and youth, but his constant exposure over the years to what was left of the Incan culture left an enduring mark upon his mind. As a result of these personal experiences, he is often his own source and his own authority.

A more fruitful source of inspiration and information was readily at hand: his mother's relatives, who had escaped Atahualpa's attempt to extirpate the royal family and who paid frequent visits to her. Their usual theme of conversation was the recollection of their golden past. They discussed the origin of their kings, their conquests and great deeds, their government and laws. From the past they would then turn to the present, lamenting the loss of their king, the end of their empire and their own reduced state. Garcilaso relates how as a child he would be in and out of the room where the remnants of royalty were gathered and would listen to parts of the conversation, entranced as children are when they listen to fables. As he grew older, his interest became more intelligent; he listened more carefully and began to question his relatives about their past. This valuable source of information was not entirely lost when Garcilaso went to Spain; his mother's brother corresponded with him after Garcilaso left Peru. Garcilaso's mother and her brother were children at the time of Atahualpa's massacre and could, therefore, have had comparatively little meaningful experience of the empire before it fell; many of those who visited the house in Cuzco were of an older generation whose testimony, though undoubtedly prejudiced, was based on wider knowledge.

When the idea of a history of the Incas began to take form in Garcilaso's mind, he realized he could not depend upon his own memory of what he had seen and heard years before. He wrote to his former mestizo schoolmates in Cuzco, asking them to gather from their mothers and Indian relatives everything that could be useful to him. The Indians, greatly pleased that an Indian planned to write their history, supplied him with such copious accounts that he had a record of the reign of each Inca and information on the various provinces that made up the empire.

Garcilaso's most important written source was a fragment of a history of Peru written in Latin by Father Blas Valera, a Jesuit. No trace of the history remains today except for the fragments translated by Garcilaso and incorporated into the *Comentarios*. According to Garcilaso, the greater part of Valera's work was lost during the English raid on the harbor of Cádiz in 1596; Garcilaso had access to the surviving portions of it through the courtesy of Father Pedro Maldonado, another Jesuit, who was teaching Scripture in Córdoba in 1600. The implication is that Garcilaso received the papers in that year. Aside from what Garcilaso tells about the manuscript—that it was most elegantly written and that the better part was missing when it came into his hands—nothing is known of the work. It was not listed in the inventories made at the time of Garcilaso's death; perhaps it was returned to Father Maldonado after the completion of the *Comentarios*. Whatever the history of Valera was, Garcilaso cites it constantly and, to judge from the use he made of it, found Valera's point of view a sympathetic one.

In keeping with his announced intention of amplifying and correcting already published histories of Peru, Garcilaso cites in the course of the *Comentarios,* the *Historia general de las Indias* of Francisco López de Gómara, the *Historia natural y moral del Nuevo Mundo* of José de Acosta, Pedro Cieza de León's *Crónica del Perú,* Agustín de Zárate's *Historia del descubrimiento y conquista de la provincia del Perú.* Less frequently mentioned are Diego Fernández' *Historia del Perú* and Jerónimo de Román's *Repúblicas del mundo.* Alonso de Ercilla y Zúñiga's epic, *La araucana,* is also mentioned briefly.

Fundamentally, the story Garcilaso had to tell was not new to the Spanish public; the list of published sources of which he made varying use indicates that the history of Tahuantinsuyu had already been told in detail and from a number of points of view. Garcilaso's task was not to tell a new story, but to correct an old one. In doing so he adds something quite different from anything contained in other historians' accounts. Garcilaso has a personal involvement in his material and it is that personal involvement that gives the *Comentarios reales* the particular quality that makes it so attractive to twentieth-century readers.

In many ways Garcilaso's claim to more intimate knowledge of the Incan empire is valid, but, from the historian's point of view, he is at the same time hampered by the sources available for his work. Since the Incas had no written records and the *quipu* was useful only for recording numbers, he was forced to depend upon the memories his Indian relatives had of the traditions of their people. The accounts sent him by his former schoolmates must have been recorded forty or fifty years after the conquest by a generation that had little personal knowledge of conditions before the fall of the empire. He had his own observations, but they were of limited use; he could describe Indian customs as he had witnessed them, altered by time and by contact with Spanish ways. He had the written records of Spanish historians, but with them he found himself in a peculiar position. One of his prime purposes in writing the *Comentarios* was to correct what he considered to be the errors of Spanish writers, yet he had to depend upon them for information and support.

In the *Comentarios,* Garcilaso was essentially dealing with two kinds of history, cultural and political or military. The framework of the history is the succession of the Inca kings beginning with Manco Capac and ending with Huascar and Atahualpa. Interspersed are chapters on nearly every aspect of human activity, from the manufacture of clothing to the rites connected with the worship of the sun. There is no apparent plan in the order in which the various cultural topics are introduced; the discussions are general statements of customs usually made without reference to time, although occasionally Garcilaso does recognize that such things may undergo changes. He is more likely to recognize differences on the basis of place rather than of time. Garcilaso explains his reasons for interrupting his chronological order, "And so that the history will not tire so much by speaking always about the same thing, it will be well to interweave in the lives of the Inca kings some of their customs which will be more pleasing to hear than the wars and conquests, almost all of them carried out in the same fashion." (II, 20)

V *Garcilaso's View of the Incan Civilization*

Garcilaso was a prejudiced historian. He believed that the Incan civilization was but little inferior to the Roman; he leaves the impression that, with one important exception, it was not at all inferior to the Spanish culture that was imposed upon it. The one serious flaw was religion, and even in that the Incas were fumbling their way toward a concept of the true God. He takes every opportunity to emphasize the highly developed social organization of Tahuantinsuyu and the excellent qualities of its people. In his special pleading he uses whatever literary devices and techniques he has to drive home his point. He does, in fact, risk overstating the case, so overwhelming is his eloquence in giving the Spanish public what he was convinced was a true picture of Peru before it was ruined and, paradoxically, saved by Spain.

The society portrayed in the *Comentarios* is a highly idealized one in which its members lived happily together. Garcilaso would have his readers believe that peace and harmony were the standard, that domestic dissension was all but unknown, that crime was non-existent, that industry was the usual thing. This theme of the ideal society relates the *Comentarios* to an idea that was highly popular in Garcilaso's day. One of the forms taken was the description of an unrealized state in which the inhabitants live under such perfect conditions that there are no social, political or economic problems. The idea was an old one; it appears in Plato's *Timaeus* and *Republic*, and in his life of Lycurgus Plutarch gives a description of Sparta that approaches the ideal. It was Sir Thomas More's *Utopia*, first published in Latin in 1516, that set the fashion for works of this sort. Francis Bacon's *New Atlantis* (1626), Tommaso Campanella's *Civitas solis* (1623), and James Harrington's *Oceana* (1656), among many others, are all reflections of man's desire to establish a kind of earthly paradise. Not all the manifestations of utopianism were theoretical, literary works. Attempts were made in America to translate theory into reality; Vasco de Quiroga, the Bishop of Michoacán in Mexico, sought to make practical application of More's social and political philosophy. The utopias in a sense looked forward to the attainment of social perfection; another tradition looked backward to a golden age in the past before society was corrupted. It is with the legend of a golden age that Garcilaso's work is most closely related. While he undoubtedly would have liked to see a future kingdom like those described in the utopian tradition, he did not have to depend upon some fictional creation of an ideal state. For him the near perfect state was fact, not legend; he needed only to listen to his elders with their melancholy, nostalgic stories of the immediate past to conclude that utopia had only recently vanished.

Garcilaso's best demonstration of the great advantages of Incan government comes from a description of the condition of the Indians before the first Inca, Manco Capac, was sent to lead them out of darkness. Garcilaso gives a picture of mankind in a state of savagery that contrasts sharply with what followed. People lived like beasts. Their religion was abominable, they worshipped all manner of plants, animals and minerals. No animal was too base and vile, says Garcilaso, for the wretched Indians to make a god of it. Their attitudes toward some of their gods were foolish; if they met a lion they were more likely to fall down and adore it than to defend themselves against the attacks of the beast. They worshipped only the concrete and visible, and that in infinite variety. Their sacrifices were often loathesome; when they made human sacrifices, they did not confine themselves to their captured enemies, but often made their own children their victims. Cannibalism was common among them. When they did band together in villages, it was without order; their huts were haphazardly grouped without streets or any other useful arrangement. Those who did not live in groups lived scattered about the hills and valleys, some in hovels, some in caves and some in hollow trees. Most of them had no notion of the domestic arts; if they clothed themselves at all, it was with the skins of animals. They did not cultivate the land, but ate herbs and roots as they found them. The family did not exist for them. Such was the state of man when the sun, in the words of Garcilaso's uncle, "sent from heaven to earth his son and daughter in order that they might teach them about our father the sun, so that they might adore him and consider him their god, and in order that they might give them precepts and laws under which they could live like reasonable, civilized men; so that they might live in houses and in towns and learn to till the fields, cultivate plants and grains, raise livestock and enjoy them and the fruits of the earth like rational men and not beasts." (I, 15)

According to the legend, Manco Capac and his queen made their first converts by preaching and by example; as word of the marvels promised by the children of the sun spread and others joined, Cuzco was founded. In the new society all were absolute equals, the only difference being that those who lived in Upper Cuzco had been recruited by Manco Capac and those who lived in Lower Cuzco were the followers of the queen. Gentleness and kindness were characteristic of Manco Capac; he established the empire and began its modest expansion by persuasion and not by force. There is a suggestion in the story told by Garcilaso's uncle that Manco Capac had grasped the idea that military strength was a useful thing to have; after the first six or seven years the Inca had an army ready to defend him and to convince those who did not join him willingly.

As he gathered in the benighted Indians, Manco Capac taught them civilized ways. He persuaded them that they should live together peacefully, without anger and passion. Each should do unto others as he would have others do unto him, since there was but one law for all. They were to respect wives and daughters. Adultery, murder, and theft were punishable by death. Each was to have only one wife who should be a member of the husband's family in order to keep blood lines pure. They were taught to weave cloth and to make shoes. From each group a *curaca* or chief was appointed who was to teach his charges like a father and who was to be obeyed like a father. Communal storehouses were established so that all would have food. The Inca established a temple for the sun and taught his subjects the proper forms of worship, how to give thanks for all the favors received. He ordered a house for the virgins to be built.

Manco Capac thus established the pattern for a benevolent, paternalistic government which was to be followed in essence by all the Incas who followed him. As Garcilaso says, "And because all the deeds of this first Inca are the beginnings and foundation of the history we are to write, it will be worth our while to relate them here, at least the most important, so that we will not repeat them in the lives and deeds of each of the Incas his descendants; because they all, kings and non-kings, prided themselves on imitating in all ways the condition, works and customs of this first Inca Manco Capac; and his history having been told, we will have told that of them all." (I, 19)

Garcilaso does not make clear whether Manco Capac used his military strength for conquest; if he did not, it was not long before his heirs realized the advantages of a good army and forgot the advice given by Manco Capac on his deathbed when he told them to attract new subjects with the benefits offered and not by force since those who were forced would never be good vassals. It is made quite evident in the histories of all the Incas up to Atahualpa that the standard procedure was first to attract new people by example so they themselves sought to unite with Tahuantinsuyu. If they showed no interest on their own, the Incas attempted to win them with reason and with promises; if they persisted in ignoring the advantages of becoming vassals of the Inca, in spite of an army drawn up on their borders, sterner measures were taken. Rarely did an Inca adopt the attitude of Mayta Capac, who on one occasion ordered his captains to avoid battle with the enemy; if they found some who were so stubborn that they would yield only to force of arms, they should be left because the barbarians lost more by resisting the Inca than he gained by forcing them.

With every Inca, conquest was a means for carrying out the commands of the sun to Manco Capac. The aim was always to civilize the unfortunates who were living without benefit of the superior

Incan culture. The statement of motive ascribed to Inca Yupanqui is typical ". . . to conquer the nations that were in that area in order to bring them into his empire and away from the barbaric and inhuman customs they had, and to give them knowledge of his father the sun so they might worship him as their god as had done the other nations that the Incas had conquered." (VII, 13)

The account of Mayta Capac's reign in Book III, Chapter 4, contains an excellent example of Garcilaso's decidedly favorable view of the conquests made by the early Incas. First, certain groups yielded willingly and graciously to the Inca; they were rewarded properly by mercies and favors. Others did not see the light quite so quickly, and it was necessary to besiege them. It was, however, a model siege, for there were no attacks despite the fact that the fortress was weak. The Inca's armies generously supplied the children of the besieged with food for themselves and enough to carry back to their elders. Sweet reason finally prevailed, and the stubborn enemies of the empire realized that if they were so generously treated while opposing the Inca, how much more so must they be dealt with if they showed themselves submissive and obedient. With this thought they capitulated and were not disappointed. The Inca's soldiers supplied them with food and clothing, always reminding them that since the Inca was the son of the sun, his only purpose was to do good to the inhabitants of the land, and not to tyrannize over them, for such was the command of his father the sun.

No matter what the manner of conquest, by persuasion or by force, the Incas, with exceedingly rare exceptions, showed a generosity and forgiving spirit that would have served as example for Christian princes. Love for his subjects was always characteristic of the Inca. His new subjects were taught to live together, they were given clothing and other gifts, they were instructed in agricultural methods. Where they were lacking, the Inca immediately constructed irrigation canals, roads, bridges, granaries, and other necessary public buildings. Most important of all the benefits, however, was the indoctrination of the newly conquered in the worship of the sun.

The constant reiteration of the noble motives of the Incas in pursuing their conquests, and the magnanimity they showed toward the conquered, make it appear that Garcilaso thought the Incas were godlike, endowed with qualities far beyond human attainment. He is not so entranced by their glories nor so blinded by his admiration that he loses all awareness of baser human motives, even in the

Incas. In connection with the gentle Mayta Capac, Garcilaso remarks that the Incas often covered their greed for increasing their land under the cloak of a desire to bring the barbarians to religion. The Inca Yupanqui set out on a campaign of conquest "as much because of the glory of expanding his empire as because of yielding to the ambition and greed for ruling, which is so natural in powerful men." (VII, 17) Tupac Yupanqui raised an army of forty thousand for a campaign whose true motive, ambition, was hidden by the veil of his zeal for the welfare of the barbarians. Still, Tupac Yupanqui must have convinced himself that conquest was a favor to the conquered. After a particularly difficult and bloody campaign, he returned to Cuzco exhausted and angry, with the remark that if the provinces next to be conquered did not take a lesson from the stubbornness of the provinces just conquered, "he would postpone subduing them for the time being and await a time when they were more disposed to accept the empire of the Incas." (VIII, 4)

Whether they were conquered from base or noble motives, the Incas' new subjects almost invariably accepted their new ways with great contentment and considered themselves fortunate to have received the many benefits of the Incan society. Such attitudes are not surprising in those who joined willingly; in those who yielded only after considerable resistance, the Incas must have considered it a mark of true enlightenment.

Garcilaso has been criticized for his failure to recognize the existence of native cultures other than the Incan, and for having taken no notice of what the Incas adopted from the people they conquered. He has been accused of lack of sympathy for the conquered Indians, and there can be no doubt but that their trials and tribulations seem to have affected him but little. Garcilaso, like the Greeks in their attitude toward the non-Greeks, looked upon most of the people conquered by the Incas as barbarians. He grants them few, if any, redeeming features. The most that could be said in favor of the best of them was that they were intelligent enough to see that the Incas possessed a superior and far more desirable culture. For Garcilaso the barbaric conditions that existed at the time of Manco Capac's coming did not alter greatly during the hundreds of years in which the Incas were making constant progress. From the first Inca to the last, many of the people they conquered were living very much as the Incas had before their enlightenment.

Some were easy for the Incas to subdue because they lived without organization, order or law. Some lived like beasts, governed tyrannically by the strongest among them. Some were exceedingly simple and gullible, ready to believe whatever they were told. There were groups that were so devoted to quarrelling and making war that no civilization was possible among them. Lack of military discipline caused the deaths of more than six thousand of one province when the Inca loss was only five hundred because of their superior training. That they lived like animals, scattered about the countryside without leaders, is a constantly recurring theme. Human sacrifice and cannibalism were frequently found among the enemies of the Incas. On all sides, the Indians continued to worship false gods, which led to immoral practices of all kinds.

If Garcilaso was something less than an objective recorder of conditions outside the Incan empire, the reasons for it are not difficult to find. It is highly unlikely that there was in his day much information available about the provinces conquered by the Incas. He cannot be held responsible for what modern archeologists and anthropologists have discovered about the cultures developed before the Incas and those contemporary with them. The information that he had came to him in the form of tradition, filtered through generations of conscious or unconscious editing by the Incas who would have been even more extraordinary than Garcilaso portrays them if they had not preserved the account of events most flattering to them.

While it is true that for the most part Garcilaso ignored the cultures of the groups that came into contact with the Incas, he was not totally unaware of the existence of culture among them, nor was he unaware that the delights of Incan civilization were not universally acceptable to the heathen. The Huancas, for example, who were conquered by Pachacutec, are described as being advanced even in religion. By implication he admits social organizations in the provinces of Chuncuri, Pucuna, and Muyumuyu which resisted Inca Roca because they refused to give up their own gods, laws, and customs. The people of Casa, Ayahuaca, and Callua, provinces in the path of Tupac Yupanqui, had an advanced political organization; they met to deal with matters of common concern, to elect governors and military leaders. Garcilaso is conscious of a certain independent spirit among some of the candidates for salvation. When Mayta Capac approached the town of Cac-yauiri, he sent the usual message to the inhabitants, informing them that he had come to improve their way of life and to bring them the benefits commanded by the sun. The Indians replied that "they had a good way of life which they did not wish to improve, that they had their gods, one of whom was yonder hill that protected them and would favor them; that the Incas should depart in peace and teach others whatever they wanted, for they did not wish to learn." (III, 2)

In Chapter 26 of Book III, Garcilaso's account of the brave Huancohuallu, who had led an abortive revolt against the great Viracocha, and his decision to depart from the Incan territory after having enjoyed nine or ten years of the gentle government of the Inca, displays a sympathy and understanding of the proud spirit of the conquered barbarian. According to Garcilaso, during those years Huancohuallu had received all the good treatment possible from the Inca. But in spite of that, "his proud and generous spirit could not suffer being the subject and vassal of another having been the absolute lord of as many vassals as he had." He found it especially hard to be reduced to the same status as the Quechuas who had been the first to reveal to the Inca Huancohuallu's plot and who had forestalled the success of his rebellion. He could not bear to be the equal of those whom he considered his inferiors. In spite of the kindly treatment of the Inca, Huancohuallu felt "and with good reason, that because of that service which his enemies had rendered to the Inca they were more beloved and esteemed than he and that he must day by day become less and less." Overcome by these thoughts, and despite his observation of the advantages of the Inca government, he desired most of all to regain his liberty. With this in mind, he sent his subjects off a few at a time with the promise that he would soon join them. He had no desire to show himself ungrateful for the favors of the Inca, nor did he wish to become a traitor to one who had been so magnanimous. He had no thought of stirring up a new rebellion for he knew it could not succeed. He contented himself with seeking his liberty "with the least offense possible toward a prince as good as the Inca Viracocha." He thus persuaded many of his former subjects to accompany him; with them he departed the Incan territories and did not stop until he was far removed from Incan influence. Finally he founded a new kingdom.

In contrast to the low state of civilization among the provinces on their borders, the Incas refined and improved their own culture with each succeeding reign. Their worship of the sun had given them an initial advantage; as they made use of the blessings granted them, they developed a highly organized, extremely efficient state. One of the most remarkable aspects of the empire, as Garcilaso reports it, was the absolute respect for law. He creates the impression that no law was ever broken, so greatly respected was the word of the Inca. The laws were strict and the punishment for their transgression was swift and harsh. No halfway measures were used; death was the reward for criminal acts, if such should ever occur. Garcilaso would have it that the severity of the laws did not represent tyranny; the people gratefully accepted the law because it insured stability. There was no economic want in the empire; every man, woman and child was assured of the necessary food, clothing and shelter. Money was unknown and its absence prevented the growth of greed. The arts and sciences flourished. Military organization was perfected. In religion, for Garcilaso the most important aspect of man's life, the concept of Pachacamac, the unknown god, began to assume more importance until finally Huaina Capac stood in the Temple of the Sun and announced that there was another and greater god who commanded the sun.

To enhance the prestige of the empire, Garcilaso often took advantage of the great esteem for Rome that is so predominant a feature of the Renaissance. Rome was great, but had only one real advantage over Tahuantinsuyu, and that was a written language with which to preserve her history. In the question of religion, the comparisons he makes are not directly between Rome and the Incan empire. When he discusses the religious beliefs and practices of the barbarians, he often reminds his reader that it should come as no surprise that such ignorant people, deprived of the advantages of civilization, worshipped so many gods. After all, the Greeks and Romans who were so advanced in other ways worshipped a great many gods. For all their depravity, the Andean barbarians did not go so far as the ancients, for they did not worship crimes and indecencies as did the Greeks and Romans with the adulterers, murderers and drunkards of their pantheon. The myths of the barbarians were no more ridiculous than many of those invented by antiquity. These comparisons, in fact, reflect credit upon the Incas; their religion was superior to that of the others because they had discarded the many gods in favor of one and were thus much nearer to the Christian concept.

Cuzco is identified as another Rome in the Foreword, a comparison that is made several times in the course of the *Comentarios*. In Book VII, Chapter 8, Garcilaso makes a more detailed statement of the likeness between the two. Both were founded by their first kings; they were alike in the variety and number of the peoples they conquered and brought into their empires. Both Rome and Cuzco developed excellent systems of law for the good government of their empires. Cuzco's great men were no less accomplished than those of Rome, but Rome was happier in having their deeds preserved for posterity. Sometimes direct comparison is made, but at others the comparison is approached indirectly. Incan institutions are described in such a way as to remind the reader forcibly of the Roman way. The House of the Virgins in Cuzco and its similarity to the Vestal virgins has already been mentioned; the entry of a victorious prince into Cuzco was very much like a Roman triumph. With some justification, it would seem, Garcilaso says that the great fortress at Cuzco surpassed the seven wonders of the ancient world. Marvelous as they were, their builders had the advantage of machines; the Incan work was accomplished without mechanical aids either for cutting the tremendous stones or for raising them into place.

Another highly respected source for comparison was the Bible, particularly the Old Testament. Here Garcilaso is more discreet in pointing out similarities. One of the legends of the appearance of Manco Capac has it that he was one of the four men and four women who, in the beginning, came forth from an opening in a cliff. Garcilaso reports that some Spaniards maintain, on the basis of the legend, that the Indians were familiar with the story of Noah and his three sons. The belief was supported by another legend that tells how, after a flood, a man appeared at Tiahuanacu and divided the world into four parts, one of which was given to Manco Capac. These legends encouraged the belief that the Indians had some knowledge of biblical events. Garcilaso is content to mention these interpretations for whatever effect they may have; "I do not meddle in such deep matters. I relate plainly the fables that I heard in my childhood; let each take them as he wishes and give them the allegory which is most appropriate." (I, 18)

The system of decuries under which the early empire was organized bears a striking resemblance to the system adopted by Moses on the advice of Jethro. "And Moses chose able men out of all Israel, and made them heads over the people, rulers of thousands, rulers of hundreds, rulers of fifties and rulers of tens." (Exodus XIX.25) Garcilaso does not call attention to Moses when he describes the Incan organization. Neither does he point out that many of the precepts attributed to Pachacutec by Valera, listed in Book VI, Chapter 36, are very like the Ten Commandments and the other laws established in Exodus. Where Pachacutec is supposed to have said, "He who kills another without authority or justice is himself condemned to death," Exodus XXI.12 reads, "He that smiteth a man so that he die, shall be surely put to death."

No comparison was necessary to identify Pachacamac with Jehovah. From the beginning the Incas had accepted the sun as the only god they worshipped, but even with Manco Capac there was the concept of a greater one who had given the sun a preeminent place among the stars of the heavens. The creator was Pachacamac. Garcilaso says the concept was not fully developed; when the Indians were asked who Pachacamac was, they replied they did not know for they had not seen him and for that reason did not build temples for him and did not offer sacrifices to him. They worshipped him silently. They scarcely dared mention his name and when they did so, they accompanied it with the gestures they used to show the highest respect. Pachacamac was of the greatest aid when the Spaniards revealed the true God to the Indians; they accepted Him readily for they said He and Pachacamac were one and the same.

Garcilaso regretted the disappearance of the empire which had, in his view, solved so many human problems with its superb system of law and its magnificent organization. The words he quotes from his uncle could well be Garcilaso's own, "And in order not to make you weep, I have not related their history with tears of blood, shed from my eyes as I shed them in my heart because of the grief I feel at seeing our Incas gone and our empire lost." (I, 17) It was not the fact of conquest that disturbed Garcilaso. He makes perfectly clear in the course of the *Comentarios* that he accepts and approves conquest, no matter what its method, though conquest by persuasion is preferable to conquest by force. Conquest was good and even necessary in realizing God's will if it was done for the purpose of the enlightenment and advancement of the conquered. The conquests of the Incas were justifiable because, as a result, the barbarians were separated from their unfortunate customs and were taught respectable ways. Most important of all, their crude religions were replaced by the worship of the sun and they were thus one step closer to Christianity. Even when the Incas were driven by the base motives of ambition and greed, the effect of their conquests was the same.

Garcilaso, then, does not find the Spanish conquest of Peru in itself to be unjust or in any way morally wrong. He is aware that Francisco Pizarro's army did not invade the empire from purely charitable concern for the natives. But, like the Incas who effected noble ends, the Spaniards carried Christianity with them and so gave the Indians a far greater gift than the material treasure they received in return. The Spanish conquest was thus the end of a long process of preparing the Indians for salvation, a work for which, Garcilaso thinks, the Spaniards owed a great debt to the Incas. Without their having led the barbarians to the threshold of true religion, the Spanish task of physical conquest and conversion would have been much more difficult. While Christianity was the most valuable contribution of the Spaniards, there were others. Garcilaso often laments that the Incas had no system of writing and that, as a result, much of their history was lost; the Spaniards remedied the lack. During the principal Feast of the Sun it was customary for the Indians to consume great quantities of alcohol. Thanks to the good example set them, after the arrival of the Spaniards there was no drunkenness; they learned to abominate it. Skilled though they were in many ways, the Incas had to await the arrival of the Spaniards for iron tools to make many useful utensils. They had iron mines but did not know how to extract the metal from its ore. One of Garcilaso's schoolmates reported that an old Inca had told him that they would have given the Spaniards their whole treasure of gold and silver just in exchange for scissors, mirrors and combs. The Indians managed nicely with the native animals they domesticated, but these were inferior to the ones introduced from Spain: horses, cows, oxen, mules, sheep, goats, pigs, and hunting dogs. The foodstuffs imported, wheat, barley, grapes, olives, and other fruits and vegetables, were also beneficial.

The Spanish conquest did bring with it some blessings, but if it had been without unfortunate results there would have been no cause for the tears of the Indians and no reason for Garcilaso to write the book he did. Christians though they now were, all was not well with the Peruvian Indians. However, except for a few general statements, Garcilaso has very little to say about the life of the common man in the *Comentarios;* it is unlikely that he ever knew much about the conditions under which the masses lived, either before or after the Spanish conquest. His bias is aristocratic, not unnaturally, since on both sides of his family he was allied with the privileged groups. His native sources of information were anything but uneducated peasants. When Garcilaso identifies himself as an Indian, which he does frequently, he really means Inca, a title that even in the most relaxed days of the empire was reserved for the nobility and for those the Incas wished particularly to honor. It was much later that all the Indians of the old empire were referred to indiscriminately as Incas.

Garcilaso offers very little evidence of the condition of the Indians under Spanish rule, and not necessarily because he was recording the history of the pre-Hispanic period. He was not such a slave to chronology that he did not make opportunity to mention matters after the collapse of the empire. He sets the tone of nostalgia and regret early with the sorrowful conversations of his relatives. In Book IV, Chapter 13, he remarks that the Incas had no tailors or cobblers and then adds the cryptic exclamation, "Oh, how many things that there are here now were not needed for they got along without them." In reference to the area around Potosí, he says, "Although the land is so rich and abundant in gold, silver and precious stones, its natives are the poorest and most wretched people in the world." (VIII, 24) In his final chapter, Garcilaso relates that he and two other Peruvians had received a letter from the remnants of the royal Incan family requesting aid in their appeal to the Crown for relief from the taxes that were crushing them. He does not quote the letter in order "not to cause grief with what they tell of the wretchedness of their lives." If Garcilaso does not in general make explicit the unhappy fate of the Indians, there is no reason to doubt that they were in great distress. The New Laws of 1542 took official cognizance of abuses of Indian labor by the *encomenderos;* the well-intentioned attempt to protect the Indian failed in its original purpose and the provisions of the laws underwent a series of modifications not to the benefit of the natives.

VI *Criticism of the Spaniards*

Here and there in the *Comentarios* are passages in which Garcilaso states openly an unfavorable opinion of Spanish conduct in Peru. These direct criticisms deal mostly with either acts of vandalism on Incan constructions or their loss through simple neglect. Temples, bridges, canals, and fountains were all lost; the great fortress of Cuzco, whose mighty walls might have stood as a monument both to its builders and to its conquerors, was gradually dismantled because the Spaniards wanted its stones to build their houses. In some cases the Spaniards caused great hardship because they ruined pastures through lack of proper usage. Garcilaso quotes Valera at some length on the general language of Cuzco. Valera elaborates on the great advantage of the one language for the whole empire, and then remarks that Spanish neglect of that language produces a situation which makes the teaching of Christianity very difficult.

The lack of proper enthusiasm in converting the Indians was a source of major distress to Garcilaso. Since the spread of Christianity was the real justification for the conquest, and since it was, in any case, the duty of Christians to teach the heathen, the failure to meet their obligations on this score was almost unforgivable. "If the Spaniards responded to this vain belief of the Indians by telling them that the true God had sent them to free them from the tyranny of the devil, which was greater than that of Atahualpa, and preached the Holy Gospel with the example that doctrine requires, there is no doubt but that they would reap a most generous harvest. But it happened so differently, as their own histories, to which I refer, relate that it is not proper for me to say so; they will say that because I am an Indian I speak with prejudice. Although it is true that not all should be blamed, for most did their duty as good Christians; but among so simple a people as those gentiles were, one bad one destroyed more than a hundred good ones built." (V, 21)

Garcilaso's most common method, however, does not involve direct and open criticism of the way in which Spanish civilization was imposed upon the Incan. Early in the *Comentarios* he gives a statement of his intention, which is to relate plainly everything about the empire, the rites and ceremonies of its idolatrous religion, the laws and customs of its government in peace and in war ". . . without comparing any of those to other similar ones found in human and divine histories, nor to the government of our times, because all comparisons are odious. He who reads them will be able to make comparisons as he likes . . . [and] he will see many laws and customs that resemble those of our own time, he will hear of many others that are completely contrary . . ." (I, 19) With this invitation, the reader is justified in searching between the lines; Garcilaso should not be offended if his words are interpreted freely.

He seems to be concerned primarily in the *Comentarios* about conditions in Peru under Spanish rule, but it is really the whole of Spanish society that attracts his attention. In Peru the Spanish government was represented by the viceroy; the organization of the colony achieved under Francisco de Toledo, who arrived in Peru in 1569, remained essentially in force until the Peruvians won their independence in the early nineteenth century. Whether the changes established by the controversial viceroy were in fact desirable and intended for the good of the native populace is not to the point here; Garcilaso gives abundant evidence in the *Historia general del Perú* that he was no partisan of Toledo. Toledo's government, with necessary differences because of local circumstances, and the society which it sought to maintain were reflections of the civilization of Spain. The bureaucratic government of the Hapsburgs and the complex social customs of a long-established culture were transplanted to the New World. Many of the things that were wrong in the colony were wrong in Spain; most of things that were right under the Incas were wrong under the Hapsburgs. Along with a concern for unhappy conditions that existed in society generally, Garcilaso's personal situation colored his attitude toward much that he criticized. His frustrated dealings with royal officials in his unsuccessful attempt to have his claims recognized, his disillusionment with his military career and his poverty, real or imagined, must all have influenced his opinion of civilized European life.

In his idealistic account of Tahuantinsuyu, Garcilaso does not adopt the satirical method used by the authors of some utopian systems to call specific attention to needed reforms in their own states, but the mere description of an ideal state must imply a non-ideal state with which it is contrasted. The desirability of change, the hope of attaining something more satisfactory than that which exists is implicit in any utopian document. Since not even its most patriotic citizen ever considered the Hapsburg empire an ideal state, it is not too much to say that Garcilaso intended the whole Inca civilization to be compared with the Spanish, always excepting the superior claims of Spain in the matter of religion. As he himself says, comparisons are odious; he chose to make his comparisons less odious by simply pointing out the virtues of the Incas and letting the alert reader draw what conclusions he would. On the surface there was nothing but a description of the Inca system. Beneath the surface there was always the Spanish method of dealing with the same problems. It was no secret that the great Incan empire was no more; it was replaced by the Spanish. Garcilaso's method was perhaps a wise one, not so much because he would have suffered in any material way had he made direct comparisons, but his public might well have been offended and his purpose of rehabilitating the Incan tradition would therefore have been far less successful.

One of the dominant themes in the *Comentarios* is the Incan conquest of neighboring tribes. The behavior of Lloque Yupanqui, related in Book III, serves as an example of the methods employed by all the Incas with but a few notable exceptions. Like them all, he much preferred to win over the barbarians by reason and by the good example of his people; if it was necessary to resort to force he did so reluctantly. Whatever the method of conquest, the procedure after submission was the same. Any resistance was at once forgiven and the conquered were so generously treated that they gratefully accepted their new status. The Inca disbanded his army, arranged for his new subjects to be instructed in religion and other matters, and made certain that his lieutenants were governing according to his instructions. The land was redistributed according to firmly fixed principles. The Inca usually did not leave his new territory immediately, but stayed on for a time to flatter his subjects by his interest in their welfare. Whatever some of them had suffered in hunger, loss of life and property in ill-conceived resistance, it was more than compensated by their easier and more enlightened life after submission to Incan rule. If, for some misguided reason, a group within the empire rebelled, the same generosity was shown them. The chiefs of the conquered nations retained their estates, were respected and given honorable positions under the Inca; wherever local customs did not conflict with Incan ways, they were kept. Never were the armies permitted to sack the conquered areas.

Initially, the Spanish conquest did not differ basically from the Incan. Certainly the Spaniards preferred to find people who did not resist, though it may be doubted that the Spaniards were quite so hesitant to give battle as the Incas supposedly were. The Spaniards immediately made efforts to convert the Indians. It was not long before the Spanish method of colonization began to show quite a different philosophy and practice. The Indians were enslaved, their masters so intent upon making their fortunes that the royal commands regarding the treatment of the Indians were more regularly ignored than obeyed. The work of conversion and education was neglected. The warmth and generosity of the Inca and his reassuring presence among his new subjects were entirely lacking under the Spanish regime. So far as its immediate effect upon the populace was concerned, the official inquiry conducted after a viceroy left office could not replace the state visits that the Inca paid to his provinces. The contrast between the methods of the two powerful empires was sharp; the lesson for the Spaniards was that kindness and humane treatment accomplish more than cruelty and destruction.

The Spanish settlers in Peru found that labor was one of their greatest problems. Even if Spanish gentlemen had not been too dignified to perform manual labor, there would not have been enough of them in the new colony to accomplish all the tasks necessary for the exploitation of the mines and the land. They turned to the obvious source, the Indians, and revived an Incan system of forced labor to insure that as much wealth as possible was drawn out of the land. For the good of the empire under the Incas, the population might be shifted from one province to another. Garcilaso accepts the idea of transferring people from their native places. Newly conquered, fertile territories could be settled by people from other provinces. The new land was fruitful and the new inhabitants were prosperous. If a province became overpopulated, transferring a part of the population eased the strain. If the inhabitants of a newly conquered area showed themselves to be bellicose and uncooperative, moving a part of them to a better established province and moving docile, civilized people in to replace them made the civilizing process simpler. All this was done for the benefit of the Inca's subjects and care was taken not to transfer people into a climate radically different from the native one; the subjects thus did not suffer unduly. While all this operated for the well-being of the populace, the Inca too derived benefits. His income increased as his lands became more productive and his kingdom enjoyed internal peace.

Every Indian was required to make a contribution of labor in the cultivation of the lands set aside for the sun and the Inca. As Garcilaso presents it, the Indians looked upon the duty as a privilege; the Inca was not a harsh, demanding master. The working conditions were nearly ideal: the workers were not removed from their home villages, they had time and energy to maintain their own fields, they were economically well off.

The *mita*, a Spanish modification of the Incan practice, demanded of the Indians a contribution of labor, theoretically for the public welfare, but public welfare had a broad definition. In any case the *mita* worked great hardship on the Indians. They were required often to move considerable distances to their assignment, the working conditions were most unsatisfactory, no consideration was given to the effects of change of climate and living conditions. The *mita* was applied to Indians who were theoretically free; the fate of those assigned to the *encomenderos* was often worse. The Crown and its representatives did show concern about the welfare of the Indians, but the law and its observance are different matters.

The old Spanish custom of honoring the law but not obeying it was prevalent among the colonists in the New World, especially in regard to those laws whose purpose it was to protect the Indian. Respect for the law and its obedience were among the virtues of the Inca's subject. Laws were made to be observed, and their enforcement was so strict that no one dared break them. Garcilaso reports that no Inca was ever brought to justice; because of their status and training, they could do no wrong. Nor was any subject ever guilty of any offense against the Inca; again training and tradition were too strong to permit it. In Garcilaso's time no Spanish monarch was ever called to account, but disobedient subjects and officials were by no means unknown. The Incas were most observant of any laws concerning religion; the Spanish state and church required the Holy Office of the Inquisition to maintain the purity of the faith.

According to Garcilaso, the swiftness of Inca justice produced a respect for law and order and prevented crime. The Spaniards brought their crimes with them. Not only did the Incan system of justice function well in criminal matters, in civil cases the poor could depend upon prompt, just action, without endless appeals and other legalistic delays. Garcilaso undoubtedly had his own experiences fresh in mind when he described this aspect of Incan culture.

Since Garcilaso's account was directed to a Spanish public, many of the situations he describes in the Incan empire may be taken as jibes against the Spanish way of life. It would not have been necessary for him to be explicit in his comparisons. Seventeenth-century Spaniards could observe the society in which they lived and of which they were a part. When he says that gold, silver, and precious stones were not demanded as tribute by the Inca but were given to him as gifts because of their decorative value, a Spanish reader did not have to be especially acute to realize that things were different in Spain. When he remarks that there were no beggars in Peru, the Spaniard had only to look around him. No Spaniard needed to be told that the Incan custom of making official appointments because of the virtue of the candidate and not because of his influence and ability to offer bribes was not the Spanish way.

Suspicion is aroused that Garcilaso's purpose in writing the *Comentarios* was not primarily to correct comparatively minor errors of interpretation by Spanish historians, but rather, by the example of the Incan solution for social and political problems, to demonstrate that the Spanish way of dealing with those problems left something to be desired.

He may strain the credulity of his reader, but it is not a question of whether or not the nearly perfect conditions he describes truly existed. The point is that he did describe them in apparent good faith, and in so doing hoped to call attention to the far-from-perfect conditions in the Peru that he knew as a youth and heard about after he went to Spain.

VII Narrative Technique of the Comentarios

In form and composition, the *Comentarios reales* is quite different from the *Florida*. The form was dictated by the materials that went into each; in the *Florida* the cultural history of the Indians de Soto encountered was incidental to the main theme; in the *Comentarios* it was as significant as part of the whole as the narrative of the activities of the individual Incas. The *Florida* had a central character around whom something like a novel could be built. The *Comentarios* had no such person and no one climactic event that permitted the development of a dramatic or novelistic structure. Although his subject matter in the *Comentarios* did not allow the same approach as he used in the *Florida,* Garcilaso does make use of many of the same techniques and devices that gave the *Florida* so much of its charm.

The narrative core of the work is the chronological account of the reigns of the Incas from the establishment of the empire by Manco Capac, an event so distant that it had become mythical, to the victory of Atahualpa over Huascar, which had taken place during the lifetime of some of Garcilaso's informants. The history of the reigns is not presented consecutively, but is broken at irregular intervals by discussions of other aspects of Incan life. The inserted, non-narrative sections, aside from their intrinsic value in an all-inclusive history, have a literary function of their own; Garcilaso uses them, as he says, to avoid boring his readers with the details of the biographies of the Incas. They may also serve to create suspense; the narrative is interrupted at a crucial moment by a discourse on some unrelated matter, to be resumed after an interval.

Within the chapters dealing with Incan customs, he occasionally introduces materials that serve various purposes in the work. In the eighth chapter of the first book, when he is giving a geographical description of the extent of the Incan empire at its peak, he stops to tell the story of Pedro Serrano, remarking that he inserts it at that point so the chapter will not be so short. The skeptical reader may not be convinced that that is the real reason. Pedro Serrano was a kind of Robinson Crusoe, who found himself stranded on an island after a shipwreck. The story is an interesting one and contains such details as the fact that, after his return to Spain, Serrano would braid his enormous beard at night in order not to become entangled in it while he slept. Like any good writer, Garcilaso has an eye to entertaining his reader and to keeping his attention; the account of Serrano's adventures accomplishes that purpose very nicely.

Introduction of material which at first glance has little relevance can be useful in other ways. Without openly confessing it, in Book VII Garcilaso tries to gloss over the failure of the Incas in their attempted conquest of Chile. He would have it that, in order to save lives, the Incas decided to civilize only the bordering provinces so the warlike Araucos would see how much improved things were under the Incas and would yield gracefully. He then embarks upon a lengthy account of the Spanish adventures in Chile, and leaves no doubt that the Spaniards found it a most difficult task to conquer that area. The material on the Spaniards in Chile is out of place chronologically, a circumstance that did not escape Garcilaso. He excuses its inclusion on the grounds that he did not know if he would have time to report it later and in its proper place. All of which may be so, but there is another and better reason for placing it where he does. If the Inca was unsuccessful in subduing the wild Araucos, so were the mighty Spaniards; the defeat of the Inca is thus minimized. It is also possible that Garcilaso wishes to point out that the provinces unconquered by the Incas, and so unprepared for the Spaniards, offered a much greater task for the Spaniards.

To lure the reader into an acceptance of what he has to say, Garcilaso has recourse to a considerable range of techniques. In dealing with the barbarians, he makes every effort possible to demonstrate that their customs were loathsome. The description of cannibalistic practices in Book I, Chapter 12, spares the reader little. The details supplied in regard to methods and attitudes leave a proper sense of horror and revulsion. When in the following chapter he deals with the barbarians' nakedness, he assumes an air of offended morality, "because history forces me to relate it entirely and truthfully, I will beg that honest ears be closed in order not to hear this part." Equally effective in such situations is his technique of passing over unpleasantness in silence, "and it is a frightful thing to hear what they said and forecast by dreams; in order not to scandalize the public, I do not repeat what I could relate in this matter." (II, 23)

The dry, unrelieved monotony of the exposition of historical, or presumably historical, events was intolerable to Garcilaso. In the *Comentarios,* as in the *Florida,* he sharpens many of his scenes by quoting what pass for the speeches of his characters, sometimes in the guise of formal address, sometimes as informal conversations. He give his narrative a vividness and creates an illusion of reality. The quoted speeches have even less justification in the *Comentarios* than they do in the *Florida;* in the latter there was at least the possibility that Silvestre might have remembered what was said in his presence, in the *Comentarios* there was no one who could have heard the words of Tupac Yupanqui and the others.

Almost from the beginning, Garcilaso seeks to involve his reader's emotions with the laments of his Indian relatives. Emotion is not limited to the sorrow of the surviving Incas, but is frequently attributed to the people conquered by the Incas. It is noteworthy that throughout the work it is grief and sorrow, not joy, that he usually records. He portrays the state of doubt and confusion in the minds of a besieged people, "With the darkness of the night they gathered together in their lodgings where the Collas, feeling the pain of their now cold wounds and seeing those who had died, having lost the heart and courage they had had up to that point, did not know what to do nor what counsel to take; they did not have strength to free themselves by force of arms and they did not know how or where to flee, for their enemies had surrounded them and closed off the passes." (II, 6)

The mind of his subject is open to Garcilaso, and he relates the emotions, ideas, and attitudes of a figure foreign not only to seventeenth-century Spaniards, but even to his Incan contemporaries. When he tells the story of the Inca war against the great Chimu in Book VI, he reports that Chimu, thinking the Inca army was weakened and that his own victory was assured, fell into melancholy when he learned of the arrival of enemy reinforcements. He saw that his battle was lost, he sensed the weakness of spirit in his own men, his hopes were dashed. Advised by his officers to surrender, pressed by the strength of the enemy and by his own weakness, he made one final appeal for continued resistance. This last flurry of activity was as pointless as the earlier ones. With afflicted heart he accepted the terms of the Inca and surrendered.

The description of Chimu's state of mind gives the account the ring of authenticity, provided the reader can free himself of the knowledge that objectively there is not a word of truth in the story, that it is the plausible product of a literary artist's imagination.

The account of the death of the first Inca, Manco Capac, is illustrative of Garcilaso's method of handling doubtful materials. He has been dealing with legendary accounts of the establishment of the Incan society for which there is no source except the fables handed down through the generations. At the beginning of the chapter, he calls attention to this when he says that "Manco Capac reigned for many years, but they cannot say for certain how many; some say more than thirty, others more than forty." The non-historical nature of the story is very quickly lost from sight for in the same sentence he states firmly, "and when he saw himself near death, he called his children." From that point on, the deathbed scene is presented as by an eyewitness, and an eyewitness who would of necessity have been one of Manco's children since the final words to his vassals are reported in summary, and then the special advice to his children after the vassals had been dismissed is related. After a paragraph in which the custom of the Inca's marrying his sister is explained, Garcilaso returns to his narrative and once more introduces material for which there can be no documentary source. He tells of the reaction of the vassals, of the mourning, of how the body was embalmed, and of how Manco Capac was worshipped as a god, son of the sun. For all his manner of relating these events as if they were fact, Garcilaso has too much respect for documentation to leave his narrative in this condition. He immediately gives a reminder that he is dealing with legend and observes critically that Manco Capac must have been a very astute Indian who fostered the legend that he and his sister were sent by their father the sun to aid the barbarians. At the end of the chapter Garcilaso again acknowledges that he is using legends, but he gives them particular status by referring to them as historical fables.

The term historical fables reveals Garcilaso's own attitude toward such material. It may not be literally true, but it is true in spirit and so serves the historian. By modern standards it is unacceptable to introduce emotions which cannot be verified except in terms of common human experience, but the poetic truth of the account cannot be questioned. When Garcilaso says that Manco Capac's vassals wept at his death, one may doubt the historical accuracy of the statement, but not its artistic validity. Garcilaso has been seeking to establish the coming of the first Inca as a great blessing to the barbarians; in effect, the virtue of Manco Capac is confirmed when his subjects mourn his death for some months and embalm the body to keep it always with them, never to lose sight of it.

Now and again a touch of understated humor creeps into the text. The Inca Viracocha, while visiting his province of Charca, was approached by ambassadors from Tucumán who addressed him in most flattering terms. Whether or not the Inca at that moment posed a military threat to their territories, Garcilaso gives no indication. The ambassadors reported that the great fame of Incan justice had convinced the people of Tucumán that they should accept the Inca as their king. They presented gifts, knelt before the Inca, and adored him as a god and as a king. The Inca received all these manifestations of humbleness with grace and generosity, and took Tucumán under his protection. The ambassadors remained with the Inca for some days, amazed by the customs of the Court; they confessed that the ways of the Incas were according to the law of men, children of the sun, and that their own ways were those of beasts without understanding. Just before they left, they happened to mention to the Inca that there was to the southwest the great kingdom of Chile with which they had no commerce but that, according to the account given by their parents and grandparents, this kingdom was greatly in need of the civilizing influence of the Incas. They recommended the conquest of the kingdom so that its inhabitants could be informed of the religion of the Incas, adore the sun and enjoy its benefits. The Inca, good administrator that he was, ordered that note be taken of the information, gave the ambassadors permission to return home, and proceeded on his tour of inspection.

The *Comentarios reales* is the great apology for the Incas and their civilization. Its value lies not so much in the objective, historical accuracy of Garcilaso's account, judged by nineteenth- and twentieth-century standards, but in the fact that he does give an accurate account of what the Incas thought they were. The constant comparison between the Incan and European cultures in nearly all features of civilization and the parallels drawn between Incan and Hebrew tradition tend to exalt the Incan nation. They place it in a respectable position, make it understandable to seventeenth-century Spaniards who were well aware of the glory of Greece, the grandeur of Rome, and the wisdom of the ancient Hebrews.

CHAPTER 6

The Historia general del Perú

AFTER his death, Garcilaso's last work, the promised continuation of the *Comentarios reales*, was published in 1617 in Córdoba by the widow of Andrés Barrera. Its title page read: *Historia General del Perú. Trata el descubrimiento del; y como lo ganaron los españoles. Las guerras civiles que hubo entre Pizarros y Almagros, sobre la partija de la tierra. Castigo y levantamiento de tiranos: y otros sucesos particulares que en la historia se contienen. Escrita por el Inca Garcilaso de la Vega, Capitan de su majestad,* etc. (General History of Peru, dealing with its discovery, and how the Spaniards won it. The civil wars which occurred between the Pizarros and the Almagros, over the division of the land. Punishment and revolt of tyrants: and other particular events which are contained in the history. Written by the Inca Garcilaso de la Vega, His Majesty's captain, etc.).

I *Résumé*

The *Historia general* is divided into eight books. In Book I, after a brief reminder of the state of affairs at the end of the *Comentarios*, Garcilaso begins the history of the Spanish conquest with a panegyric on Francisco Pizarro and his family. This is followed by a review of the economic state of Spain before her acquisition of colonies in the New World, of the early explorations of Pizarro, and of his negotiations for permission to undertake the conquest of Peru. After his arrival and first contact with the Inca's representatives, attention is focused for the rest of the book upon Atahualpa, the familiar story of his initial disdain for the Spaniards, his capture, and finally his execution.

Book II recounts the arrival of Pedro de Alvarado, accompanied by Captain Sebastián de la Vega, the agreement made between Alvarado and Diego de Almagro, and the death of Alvarado. In

Cuzco Francisco Pizarro received a visit from Manco Inca, younger brother of Huascar, who presented his claims to the Incan throne. Pizarro, in order to keep the populace as quiet as possible, agreed to the coronation of Manco Inca, but left no doubt as to who was the true master of the empire. Manco Inca, who soon began to smart under the treatment of the Spaniards, led a rebellion during which much of Cuzco was burned. Finally realizing that defeat was inevitable, he withdrew to the remote Andes. The troubles between the Pizarros and the Almagros culminated in the execution of Diego de Almagro.

Book III continues the account of the struggle for power among the Spaniards. The younger Almagro and his followers assassinated Francisco Pizarro and found themselves in difficulty with Vaca de Castro, who had been sent from Spain to investigate the troubles in Peru. Vaca de Castro defeated and executed Almagro, ending the first phase of the civil wars. A new cause of disturbance arose, the promulgation of the New Laws.

Book IV opens with the arrival of the first viceroy, Blasco Núñez Vela, who found serious problems in the enforcement of the New Laws. Gonzalo Pizarro, who emerged as the leader of the rebellious *encomenderos*, began open warfare on the viceroy and finally entered Lima as governor. Núñez Vela was sent to Spain, but on the way was released by one of his guards. His return to Peru opened another phase of the wars which ended with the death of Núñez Vela on the battlefield. The complicated state of affairs during this period is related in great detail.

The appointment of the priest, Pedro de la Gasca, as president of the *Audiencia* begins Book V. The death of Núñez Vela had not put an end to the difficulties, though Gonzalo Pizarro was in a strong position. La Gasca's task was the same as that of his predecessors; he was more successful than they. A series of minor battles led up to the first major encounter between the two forces, the battle of Huarina, in which Pizarro was victorious. La Gasca was not deterred, but continued to pursue Pizarro whom he defeated at the battle of Sacsahuana. Both Pizarro and his chief lieutenant, Francisco de Carvajal, were executed.

La Gasca's troubles after the death of Pizarro form the first part of Book VI. His attempt to make a fair distribution of assignments of Indians for labor caused considerable dissatisfaction which erupted in a number of minor uprisings. When comparative peace was restored, La Gasca gave up his post, leaving the government in the hands of the *Audiencia*. After a short interval, the next viceroy, Antonio de Mendoza, governed briefly until his death. The *Audiencia*, against the viceroy's advice, forbade the use of Indians for personal service, a most unpopular decision which gave rise to another series of attempted rebellions. The leaders were defeated and executed.

Book VII is confined to the rebellion of Francisco Hernández Girón who opened his campaign at the wedding supper attended by Garcilaso. Affairs at this time were apparently in a state of great confusion; the *Audiencia* had extreme difficulty in settling upon a course of action to deal with the threat of Girón. In the early stages, Girón was victorious, a circumstance that only increased the discord among the royal supporters. Girón was ultimately defeated. His captors entered Lima in triumph with their prisoner, who was promptly tried and executed.

Book VIII relates the events of the administrations of the next three viceroys. Andrés Hurtado de Mendoza, Marqués de Cañete, was occupied with restoring order after Girón's rebellion. His successor, the Conde de Nieva, had an uneventful period in office. After an interval in which Peru was in the charge of a governor, Francisco de Toledo was appointed. For Garcilaso the only event of any seeming consequence was the execution of Tupac Amaru, claimant to the Inca throne, who was accused of rebellion by Toledo and executed. Garcilaso gives an account of the proceedings highly favorable to Tupac Amaru. The work ends with Toledo's return to Spain where Philip II received him with great disapproval.

II *Evolution of the* Historia

By the time he came to dedicate this final book, Garcilaso had apparently given up hope of attaining favor from earthly patrons; the *Historia* is dedicated to the Virgin Mary. The style of the dedication is for Garcilaso a strange, inflated one, filled with extravagant classical allusions in which the Virgin is "Bellona of the Church militant, Minerva of the Church triumphant." The deeds of the victorious lions of Castile are greater and more heroic than those of the Alexanders of Greece and the Caesars of Rome; the Spanish heroes are worthy of comparison with the godlike Hercules and Achilles. Buried in the elaborate prose is a statement of one of the causes that led him to write the *Historia*. "Finally, paternal devotion inherited with the nobility and name of the famous Garcilaso, Commander of the Order of Ave Maria, Spanish Mars, to whom that more than Roman triumph and victory more glorious than that of Romulus over the Moors on the plains of Toledo gave the surname of La Vega and renown equal to the Bernardos and Cids and the Nine Worthies."

At the end of the *Comentarios,* Garcilaso speaks of a tenth book which will deal with the heroic deeds of the Spaniards who won the empire; this was in March, 1604. There is no indication of when that tenth book was expanded to fill the eight books of the *Historia.* If he had not begun to write the history of the Spanish conquest in 1604, he must have done so soon after. In the *Historia* there are a few dates that indicate his progress in composition or revision. In Book VI, Chapter 6, he indicates that he is writing at the end of 1610; in the last chapter of Book VII, he mentions having received certain information in 1612. The last date he gives in the text is 1613, found in Book VIII, Chapter 20. On this last date he must have been revising the text; he had applied for a license to print the work on December 13, 1612, and in the application indicated that the work was completed, though he makes no reference to the number of books contained in it. On January 26, 1613, approval was granted for the eight books of the second part of the *Comentarios reales.* Garcilaso's agreement with Francisco Romero regarding the publication of the work was signed October 23, 1614. On October 29, 1616, the chapter of the cathedral of Córdoba authorized Andrés de Bonilla to make arrangements for the publication of the book. The title under which it finally appeared was clearly not the one given it by Garcilaso who, in his dedication and application for license, refers to it as the second part of the *Comentarios reales.*

III *Sources*

The written sources for the *Historia* are essentially the same as those for the *Comentarios,* and in parts of the *Historia* Garcilaso depends heavily upon written sources for his account. He also had the advantage of information collected from such people as Gonzalo Silvestre, whose experiences in Peru after the Florida expedition were generously shared with Garcilaso. Another extremely valuable, though no doubt prejudiced, source was Garcilaso's father and his friends. Often Garcilaso remarks that he had certain facts from his father, or that a story he has just told was exactly as he heard it from his father's friends, who were no more reluctant to reminisce than

Silvestre was. All the information from such sources was valuable, but none of it gives the *Historia* its particular value and interest; that comes from Garcilaso's own personal participation in some of the events he records, and from his having lived through the troubled but exciting period in which the authority of the Spanish government was established over the obstreperous conquerors of the Incas. In the *Florida*, Garcilaso was dealing with events in a time and place far removed from his personal experience; he depended entirely upon others for his information, and had to base his interpretation upon what he could gather from the accounts given him. In the *Comentarios* he was closer to his materials; he could look about him in his youth and observe the physical setting in which great events took place. He was exposed to legends, beliefs, and interpretations of Indians, some of whom had witnessed the last days of the Incas. But still the empire was dead when Garcilaso listened to the stories of his Indian relatives, and he did not personally share in their life under the empire. A great part of the *Historia*, on the other hand, is Garcilaso's own story by virtue of his having seen and known many of the leading characters who fill his pages. The *Comentarios* was a tribute to his mother's people; the *Historia*, as he indicates in his dedication, is a tribute to his father's.

In truth the *Comentarios* and the *Historia* are not two separate works, though there is a tendency to consider them so. They are very different, but both are necessary to Garcilaso's purpose, the description of a glorious empire, of a noble people all but destroyed by the invading Europeans. After a brief consideration of what man was before the divinely inspired message of Manco Capac was delivered, a section which is of necessity sketchy, he embarks upon the account of the organization of the Inca state. The *Comentarios* brings the story down to the arrival of the white man. The *Historia* is contemporary history, treating events which transpired within the lifetime of Garcilaso. It is the story of Spanish domination, and it ends with the accomplishments of Viceroy Toledo who, except for sporadic outbursts, effectively put an end to all Incan dreams of restoring the old government and the return of power to the hands of native Peruvians. The parts taken together form an account of the rise and fall of the Incan empire.

In some respects, the *Historia* is a more coherently organized work than either the *Florida* or the *Comentarios;* chronology is more strictly observed, perhaps because of necessity arising from the complicated history of the early years of Spanish domination.

IV *Purpose of the* Historia

The *Historia* is prefaced by an address to the Indians, mestizos, and Creoles of Peru; it is a document of considerable interest because in it Garcilaso sums up his purposes in writing the two parts of the *Comentarios reales,* and because he gives his ideas on the uses of history. His first reason for writing was a patriotic one, to make Peru known to the rest of the world, to show that it is now as rich in its wisdom and knowledge of God and His Law as it was before in gold and silver. He praises the quick, able minds of his countrymen, and exhorts them to make good use of their natural abilities, to pursue their intellectual development in order to show the Old World that the New is not barbaric. It should be a matter of pride to Spain, Garcilaso says, that she was chosen to bring Christianity to those heathen who are now members of the Christian republic.

The second motive in writing his history was to celebrate the greatness of the heroic Spaniards who "with their valor and military skill won for God, for their king, and for themselves that rich empire whose names, worthy of cedar, live in the book of life and will live immortal in the memory of mortals." He then gives three reasons for recording the deeds of men distinguished in arms and letters. First, it is to reward their merit with undying fame. Second, it is to honor the nation. Last, and perhaps most important, it is to offer an example to posterity so that by studying the past, victory will be attained in the future. Garcilaso aims to accomplish all three purposes in his histories, but he dwells at greater length on his hopes that the new generation, by emulating those who converted Peru, Chile, Paraguay, Mexico, and the Philippines, will do the same in Florida and in the Magellanic territories.

His third reason for writing was to make good use of his time, not to waste it in pointless activities. That, he says, led him to write the *Florida* and to translate León Hebreo's dialogues.

V *Garcilaso's View of the Spanish Conquest of Peru*

One need read only the preface to the *History* to be completely convinced, if he were not before, that the only justification needed for the Spanish conquest of the New World was the Christianization of the natives. So much does Garcilaso insist upon the theme in all his works that it becomes almost obsessive. Throughout the *Comentarios* he approves the Incan conquests because, as a result, the Indians were more enlightened than before; in the *Historia* it is the

Spaniards whose actions, cruel at times, are worthy because they brought final enlightenment to the Indians.

It was not entirely the wisdom and convictions of either Inca or Spaniard that were fundamentally responsible for the good work they accomplished. Beginning with the legend of Manco Capac, there is introduced the basic cause of all the good that was done: God took pity upon the barbarians and sent Manco Capac to lead them. The conviction that, in exercising their influence over barbarians, the Incas were unknowingly doing God's work shows through in many passages of the *Comentarios*. The Incas were successful because they were moving in the right direction, preparing the natives to accept Christianity.

If the Incas received credit in Garcilaso's eyes for furthering the cause of true religion, the Spaniards received even more. The providentialism seen in the *Comentarios* is even more directly stated, and more dominant, in the *Historia*. Signs of divine mercy and of God's guidance of human affairs are evident throughout, but most particularly so in the first two books. One of the first signs of the working of God's will occurred during Pizarro's preliminary explorations. The Spaniards landed at Tumpiz and were curious about the place; Pedro de Candía, armed with Christian faith and conviction, clothed from head to foot in armor and carrying a crucifix, set out to explore. The natives were dumbfounded at the sight as Candía marched into their town and sent against him a lion and a tiger. Contrary to expectation, when the two beasts saw the crucifix, they lost all their fierceness and fell down at Candía's feet as though they were dogs. The natives, seeing the effect of the cross on wild animals, concluded that the strange figure was sent from heaven; they showed him all their immense treasure, which astounded Candía more than his appearance impressed the Indians. His report to his companions was so glowing that they decided then and there to return to Panama to make arrangements for a greater expedition, which eventually brought the Cross to all of Peru.

In his first chapter, Garcilaso explains how marvelous it was that the three original partners in the conquest undertook such a task, and then adds, "But the principal thing was that God had mercy on those gentiles and wished in this way to send them His Gospel, as we will see in the many miracles He performed in their favor during the conquest." The strength and courage of the Spaniards for the difficult tasks of the conquest were the gift of divine mercy. In all they suffered from hunger, thirst, and exhaustion, they were sustained by God. It was again God's will that Atahualpa became so dispirited and intimidated that "he neither resisted nor used the power that he had against the Spaniards; but when we consider it carefully, it was the punishment for his idolatry and cruelty; and besides it was the work of divine mercy for bringing those gentiles to the Roman Catholic Church." (I, 17) Atahualpa's death was punishment from heaven, for God lets those who place their faith in tricks and in tyranny fall into their own traps.

The siege of Cuzco during the rebellion of Manco Inca was particularly fruitful in signs for the Spaniards that God had approved their cause. The first indication of divine favor came when the Indians set fire to the palace of the Inca Viracocha where the Spaniards were lodged. The whole building was destroyed except for one large room in which the Spaniards had their chapel. This, according to Garcilaso, God spared from the fire; wherever the Indians managed to shoot their flaming arrows, the fires were immediately extinguished as though water were thrown on them. Another miracle, even more impressive to Spaniard and Indian alike, was the appearance of St. James, patron of Spain, who manifested himself to fight alongside the Spaniards at a particularly crucial moment in the siege. Though greatly amazed, the Indians persisted in their attempt to dislodge the Spaniards. At this point, a third miracle occurred, the apparition of the Virgin with the Child Jesus in her arms. The Indians were so astonished and stricken with fear that their attacks thereafter were lacking in the enthusiasm necessary to carry them to the victory they had every reason to expect.

With such evidence that the conquest of the Incan empire was an undertaking carried out under divine sponsorship, it is but a step to assume that whatever material wealth the Spaniards found was but a just reward for their sacrifices in bringing Christianity to the heathen, and that it was the duty of those saved to serve their conquerors. There was always, to be sure, the obligation of the Christian to do everything possible to ensure that proper instruction was given the new converts.

VI Indian and Spanish Figures of the Conquest

The *Historia* is not a cultural history; it is the story of a group of individuals who found themselves in conflict; first Spaniard against Indian, and then Spaniard against Spaniard. Except for the masses of Indians and a number of unnamed Spaniards who had their comparatively minor roles in the struggle, Garcilaso develops his account in terms of the actions of specific persons rather than as an exposition of general political and economic principles that guided events. Such a method was impossible for the *Comentarios,* except for the limited information he was able to gather concerning the individual Incas; he had to confine himself to more general statements about the civilization. With the beginning of the Spanish conquest, the participants, both Indian and Spanish, stand in sharp relief. From Garcilaso's portrayal of these men, and from his attitudes toward them, it is possible to draw some conclusions in regard to his stand on broader issues.

The identifiable Indians who play any significant part in the history of Peru after the arrival of the Spaniards are few. Huascar and Atahualpa were the leading figures in the early stages of the conquest. Garcilaso's strong prejudice in favor of Huascar, the legitimate heir betrayed by his half-brother, was probably inherited from his mother and her family who were so cruelly treated in the struggle for power. Huascar remained the gentle, noble Inca, perhaps lacking in resolution, but nonetheless a ruler in the great Incan tradition. Atahualpa was exactly the opposite, a usurper, a tyrant, a brutal murderer. Here again Garcilaso's opinion derived from the strong feelings of his Indian family. According to Garcilaso, Atahualpa wished to be buried in Quito with his maternal ancestors rather than in Cuzco as would have been proper for a legitimate Inca; he knew how much hatred had been aroused in the empire because of his cruelty, and feared that a tomb in Cuzco would be defiled. Garcilaso makes some effort at a balanced judgment, but his aversion to the tyrant makes his attempt unconvincing. "That an idolatrous Indian who had committed so many cruel acts as Atahualpa should be baptized, we should give thanks to God our Lord who does not cast out of His infinite mercy such great sinners as he and I." (I, 36)

Two other royal Incas, claimants to the throne, appear in the *Historia.* Manco Inca, in whom Pizarro saw a tool for governing the Indians, seems naive; he was certainly inexperienced in the ways of the western world. It was his belief that reason and justice would prevail, and that his claims would be recognized. "Let us go there armed with a just request; let us expect more from the rectitude of those whom we consider gods than from our own actions; for if they are true sons of the sun as we believe, they will act like Incas: they will give us our empire." (II, 11) His hopes for receiving the traditional *borla* were not disappointed, but he soon became aware of how much he had been deceived in other respects. His rebellion placed him on the wrong side, and because of that his failure was assured. Garcilaso still treats him sympathetically. In the long speech to his captains, in which Manco Inca announces his intention to give up the struggle, it is apparent that he recognizes the miraculous appearance of the Virgin as a sign from Pachacamac. He urges his people to accept the Spaniards and to live in peace with them. In his exile he will be content with the knowledge that all goes well under the Spanish government.

Tupac Amaru, son of Manco Inca, was accused by Viceroy Toledo of a treasonable attempt to establish himself as legitimate ruler of the Indians.[1] Garcilaso's sympathies are all with the Inca, whom he portrays as an innocent youth living peacefully in the mountains with no ambition for power. Toledo, fearful that this last unconverted scion of the royal house would be a source of trouble, trumped up a series of charges and seized the prince. Tupac Amaru, in the mistaken belief that his innocence would protect him, gave himself up to the soldiers sent to arrest him. He was sentenced to death; thirty-six of his male relatives were confined to Lima, where they could be kept under surveillance. For Garcilaso, Tupac Amaru was the victim of the viceroy's unreasoning hatred; Spaniards and Indians were shocked at the cruel, inhuman treatment given him. He conducted himself nobly, accepted baptism, and died like a great prince.

For the first conquerors of Peru, Garcilaso displays the most extravagant admiration. In his second chapter, he compares Francisco Pizarro, Diego de Almagro and Hernando de Luque to the second Roman triumvirate, and not to the advantage of the Romans. The Romans were tyrants, looking only to their own advantage, and divided the empire among themselves. The Spaniards were generous, dedicated, not to the destruction of the Spanish empire, but rather to its increase; they labored for the good of others.

Francisco Pizarro, who has enjoyed a reputation as one of the cruelest of Spanish conquerors, emerges from Garcilaso's pages as a true Christian hero. His devotion to the Crown and the Cross was exemplary; a rich man when the conquest was undertaken, he died poor. His nature was so bland and affable that he never had an unkind word for anyone. He was a simple, unsophisticated man; his generosity towards his men earned their greatest respect and admiration. He was a prince, and more. Garcilaso betrays his attitude toward the hero when he objects to other historians having referred to Pizarro's illegitimate birth and his early career as a swine-

herd. In the lives of those worthy of fame, such things should not
be spoken of, even if they are true.

Diego de Almagro's difficulties with the Pizarros did nothing to
lessen Garcilaso's admiration for his sterling qualities. Poisonous
tongues sought to defame the great soldier with unkind references
to his birth. But for Garcilaso, illegitimacy was no cause for scorn;
he took the position that sons of unknown fathers should be judged
by their own deeds. On that score, Almagro's accomplishments made
him well born. He died in misfortune, but the memory of his heroic
works survived. His mestizo son, who assassinated Francisco Pizarro
avenge his father's death and who was himself executed, was
like his father. They had the same spirit and courage in war,
same prudence in peace. Almagro the younger would have been
best mestizo born in the New World had he only obeyed the
ister of his King.

Garcilaso was a strong partisan of Gonzalo Pizarro, perhaps partly
because of his father's close association with the great man, and
perhaps partly because of Garcilaso's own acquaintance with him.
He is pictured as a man of noble spirit, incapable of malice, with no
talent for trickery and deception. He was himself truthful and of
so trusting a nature that he believed what his friends, or those who
passed for such, told him. That was the cause of his downfall. It was
not true, Garcilaso insists, that he was not very intelligent, as some
of his detractors claimed. Like his brother, he had been a rich man,
but he died in poverty, in part because he was so generous with his
wealth. He never refused a request. His generosity was not confined
to material goods; his lieutenants saw to it that no man condemned
to a just death ever had opportunity to appeal to Gonzalo Pizarro.
He could always be counted on to grant pardon.

Of the representatives of the Crown sent to restore and maintain
some semblance of order in the colony, Vaca de Castro receives
Garcilaso's full approval. A prudent man who governed justly, he
was respected by both Indians and Spaniards because of his wise
ordinances. The Indians were especially pleased because they said
that his laws were very like the laws of the Incas. Some of Garcilaso's
good opinion may be due to the fact that his father received favored
treatment in the *repartimientos* assigned by Vaca de Castro. Garcilaso is charitable to the first viceroy, Blasco Núñez Vela, but had
no high opinion of him. All the blame for the troubles of his period
in office was not his; he was merely trying to carry out the King's

instructions which were advantageous neither to the King nor to the colony. He could not be held guilty for all the deaths of Spaniards and Indians that occurred during his term. Pedro de la Gasca was praised because of having restored peace to Peru and Peru to Charles V. Antonio de Mendoza's death soon after taking office was a great loss for Peru. Andrés Hurtado de Mendoza was a harsh governor, though at the end of his term he became much more reasonable. Garcilaso's lukewarm attitude may be due to the influence of Gonzalo Silvestre who was one of the group of troublesome, unattached soldiers who were sent back to Spain by Hurtado de Mendoza.

The last viceroy to appear in the *Historia* was Francisco de Toledo whose misfortune it was, so far as his fame and reputation are concerned, to have earned the disapproval of Garcilaso. Until the twentieth century, when some attempt has been made to reevaluate the work of Toledo in Peru on a more objective basis, he has had the popular reputation of a harsh and unjust enemy of the Indian. He was in fact probably a devoted, energetic officer of the Crown, deserving of the title sometimes given him, Solon of Peru. His theory was that so long as the old Incan customs remained, and so long as there were remnants of the royal family in locations where they could stir rebellion, the Spanish position was not secure. Though he effectively put an end to what was left of the Incan social structure, in many ways he improved the conditions under which the masses of Indians lived. None of these positive accomplishments of Toledo is to be found in the *Historia*. It has been suggested that it was the action of Toledo that inspired Garcilaso to write the *Comentarios* and the *Historia*. Be that as it may, the last chapters of the book are devoted to the story of Toledo's heartless persecution of the innocent Tupac Amaru.

Fray Bartolomé de las Casas, known throughout America as the Apostle of the Indies because of his dedication to their cause, was another who, in Garcilaso's opinion, was the cause of great injustice in the New World. Ironically, it was because the adoption of the New Laws was urged by Las Casas that Garcilaso considered him a tool of the devil. The Laws were designed to ease the lot of the Indian and to offer him some protection against the abuses of his Spanish masters, but for Garcilaso their effect was anything but desirable. He thought that their result was a weakening of efforts to convert the Indians.

Taking the *Comentarios reales* and the *Historia* as a unified whole,

[130]

as they were intended to be taken, it may seem that there is a strange contradiction in Garcilaso's impassioned defense of the Incan empire in the *Comentarios* and his strongly expressed sympathy for such men as Gonzalo Pizarro, the leader of the rebellion against the New Laws intended for the welfare of the Indian. In the *Historia,* no less than in the *Florida* and the *Comentarios,* Garcilaso insistently identifies himself as an Indian, and yet he can praise those who were instrumental in the collapse of the Indian empire and who exploited the people they conquered. The *Comentarios* is filled with criticism of the Spaniards, the *Historia* with their praise.

The fact of the Spanish conquest of the Incas cannot be a source of dissatisfaction to Garcilaso, for he recognizes that conquest is not only justifiable, but desirable if it brings with it some improvement for the conquered. The Incas based the expansion of their empire upon the command to Manco Capac that he should educate the barbarians and show them the true way. The Spaniards, to a degree at least, based their conquest on the same principle, that it was the privilege and the duty of Christians to bring the Gospel to the heathen. In his attitude toward Incan and Spanish conquests, Garcilaso shows no inconsistency.

If the Spaniards brought salvation to the Indian, and if the conquerors were the admirable people he considered them to be, there arises the question of what it was that Garcilaso found so distasteful in the Spanish regime. There is no doubt that he would have found the idea of giving up Christianity for the sake of restoring the old empire totally impossible. Yet the *Comentarios* is filled with nostalgia and regret for what was lost; true religion was a step forward, but it came at considerable cost. The *Historia* has chapters that report the oppressive conditions under which the former Incan aristocrats barely managed to survive. Garcilaso found the New Laws almost wholly intolerable; in his opinion, they so altered the system of Spanish control of land and population that the Indian was deprived of protection and, more important, of the opportunity for instruction in religion. He apparently felt, as undoubtedly his father and friends felt, that without direct responsibility for specific groups, the Spaniards would be less inclined to devote themselves to the welfare of the Indians. At its best, the original method of assigning Indians and lands to Spaniards produced a paternalistic system under which a well-intentioned master would do his full duty toward his charges.

Garcilaso's favorable bias toward the old Incan society, toward Manco Inca and Tupac Amaru, toward the Pizarros and their company, would indicate that he approved of their kind of organization. His report that Vaca de Castro was successful both with Indians and Spaniards because his laws were like the laws of the old empire and clearly acceptable to the conquerors is further evidence of Garcilaso's stand. The New Laws were a move to wipe out paternalistic government. Toledo's policy of removing Incan influence from life in the colony was the final step in the destruction of the Incan empire.

Garcilaso was not totally without concern for the material well-being of the masses, but their spiritual welfare was far more important. The aristocrats deserved respect and consideration befitting their privileged position. Christianity must be maintained and spread throughout the colony. Garcilaso's utopian dream was, in truth, the restoration of the Incan empire with Spanish governors who would continue the policies of the Incan kings without interference from well-meaning but misguided reformers and bureaucrats. He wanted the best of both worlds, a society which would benefit Indians, mestizos and Creoles, a society in which his own double heritage would be honored.

CHAPTER 7

Garcilaso as Historian and His Reputation

G ARCILASO may be criticized from the point of view of modern historiography for many of the methods, techniques, and devices he used in writing his histories. But Garcilaso was not a nineteenth- or twentieth-century man; he was a product of the Renaissance, as the contents of his library demonstrate, and it is as a Renaissance historian that he must be judged. His ideas of what was acceptable and proper in a history were those that were commonly subscribed to in the sixteenth century by humanistic theoreticians and by the practitioners of the art of historical writing.

I *Renaissance Uses of History*

With the revival of classical learning to which so much energy was devoted in the Renaissance, humanists turned their attention to the Greek and Roman historians.[1] The study of Thucydides, Herodotus, Livy, Polybius, Tacitus among the historians, of Cicero and Quintilian among the rhetoricians, began to have its effect. The analysis of the classical writers, and the comparison of their histories with medieval chronicles and annals produced a revised outlook upon the way man's experience in the past should be recorded and interpreted. History was an art as much as any other form of writing; since one of its aims was to persuade its readers, the techniques of rhetoric came into play to assure a style that would meet the demands placed upon the historian.

Out of the studies and theorizing of Machiavelli, Guicciardini, Bodin, and Robortello, among many others, there emerged a kind of standard approach to the historian's task. Although individual authors adopted varying aspects of it, what went into the composition of any particular history differed according to the specific needs, circumstances, and point of view of the author.

In general, the purposes served by history were two. The search for fame and glory preoccupied the men of the Renaissance; one of the ways to assure the attainment of these goals was through written accounts. In the rising national states, there was a strong feeling that oblivion was the fate of nations without recorded history, and no Spaniard, Italian, Frenchman, or Englishman was quite willing to see the accomplishments of his native land forgotten. The ancient Greeks, Romans, and Jews were remembered because they had written records. For the man of the Renaissance, the waters of Lethe offered no comfort.

The second use of history was to teach by example from the past. Since it was generally believed human nature does not change, men of the first century and men of the sixteenth could be expected to react to similar causes in similar ways. By the study of the past and by the careful identification of cause and effect, it was thought possible to arrive at intelligent decisions in solving social and political problems. A knowledge of the rise and fall of great nations and of the prosperous and unfavorable fortunes of great men could make the present more intelligible, and could guide those in charge of public affairs.

History, while based upon fact, became a creative art. Like the orator, the historian sought to persuade and instruct; it was no longer satisfactory to present a bare recital of facts. Cicero's requirements for a properly written history were generally accepted. The first requirement was that truth be reported impartially by the author. Events must be important ones; they must have both chronological order and be given geographical location. The persons involved in the events are to be described; some attention should be given, not only to the action itself, but to its causes and the manner in which it was realized. The style should be a pleasing one.[2]

II *Garcilaso's Intentions as Historian*

Garcilaso was acutely conscious that his labors in writing his histories of Spanish and Indian exploits in the New World would help to make the names of Spain and Peru glorious. He wrote the *Florida*, he says in his proem, because "it seemed to me an unworthy and sorry thing that such heroic works which have been done in the world should be left perpetually forgotten." The Incas' lack of a written language meant that much of their history was lost and they risked the dreaded oblivion that was the normal fate of such peoples. He was anxious to remedy this state of affairs by gathering up what was known of the Incan past, and by recording it for posterity in the *Comentarios*. The *Historia* was intended to make the kingdom of Peru known to the universe. Through it, the merit and valor of the heroes would be rewarded with the honor and praise that such virtue demands. So far as his own fame is concerned, Garcilaso hides behind the mask of a humble Indian and only very modestly calls attention to the fact that he is the author of works dedicated to the service of his country and his compatriots. For all his humility, he knew that his own name must be associated with the glories he recorded.

There is a strong didactic current in all of Garcilaso's work. The *Florida* was designed to point out that an error had been made by Spain in not pursuing the conquest of the territory, but that that error could yet be remedied. The *Comentarios reales* was to show a near ideal state in operation, to teach the Spaniards how an empire should be governed successfully and expanded. The *Historia* demonstrated that a magnificent addition to the Spanish empire was endangered because of foolish laws and inept or cruel administration of those laws. In each of the works, there are depicted the lives of great men, Spaniards and Indians, from whom much could be learned. The *Florida* offers the example of de Soto, whose noble work came to failure because of a certain weakness in his character. In the *Comentarios* there is the story of Huaina Capac whose error in dividing his kingdom was at least partly responsible for its weakened condition when the Spaniards arrived. The successful reigns of most of the Incas, their generosity, and their almost Christian treatment of those they conquered, show how a conqueror should conduct himself. In the *Historia*, the noble actions of the Pizarros in assuring the Indians of salvation are worthy of emulation.

In view of his impassioned defense of the Incas, it may seem paradoxical to insist upon Garcilaso's impartiality. He had preconceived ideas about the nobility of the Incas, about their empire, and about their fate. He had prejudices in favor of his father's companions and against Viceroy Toledo. In spite of all that, Garcilaso thought he was a well-balanced, impartial recorder of the history of the rise and fall of the Incan empire. He may have been guilty of self-deception, but unless he is to be accused of conscious and deliberate falsification, his claims to freedom from prejudice must be accepted as sincere. "I promise that my affection for them will be no cause for failing to state the truth of the facts, omitting nothing of the bad or adding anything of the good which they had." (*Comentarios*, I, 19) He quoted freely from earlier Spanish historians, not only to take exception to their statements of fact and their interpretations. They were a source of authority for him, and he cites them freely and frequently in support of his own statements; they offered protection against the charge of prejudice. That he thought he was impartial is the important thing in judging him as an historian. The fact that he was not impartial does not entirely invalidate his history; his prejudices are obvious to his reader, and they reveal the man himself, and an attitude toward the history he records.

The question of truth in history is a difficult one. For the Renaissance historian, as for the classical historian, truth was not necessarily scientific truth; it is on this rock that so many sixteenth-century histories founder today. Truth, if it is once identified, may be expressed in many forms. Since history in the Renaissance was to be presented as continuous, coherent narrative, and was to demonstrate guiding principles in the life of man, it was quite acceptable if the historian saw fit to rearrange the order of facts to make more meaningful associations, or if he saw fit for his purpose to omit some facts altogether. The important thing was that the greater truth, the coherence and order of public affairs, should be arrived at. The spirit of the truth had to be represented through a judicious selection and arrangement of factual material.

Garcilaso was no less devoted to truth than any of his contemporaries. With the proem to his first historical work, the *Florida,* he announces his intention of stating the truth of what occurred during de Soto's expedition; he states that his main source was trustworthy and devoted to speaking the truth. Further, to ensure accuracy, he checked Silvestre's account against whatever other sources were available. Similar protestations about his devotion to truth and his intention to be guided by it and confined to it are found in many pages of the *Comentarios* and the *Historia.*

III   *Garcilaso's Method as Historian*

Garcilaso takes advantage of his privilege to select and arrange his facts in order to produce a narrative adequate to his purpose. In the *Comentarios,* Chapter 19 of Book I stands as a justification and explanation of his method. "We will give attention to reporting the most historical deeds, leaving out many others as being non-pertinent and prolix; and although some of the things that have been said and others that will be said may seem fabulous, it seemed best to me not to omit them nor to remove the foundations upon which the Indians base the best and greatest things they relate about their empire. . . . Therefore it will be permitted for me to say what is fitting for the best account that can be given of the beginning, middle and end of that monarchy."

One of the characteristics of all of Garcilaso's histories is his custom of attributing to his characters speeches which they could not conceivably have made and of recording dialogues for which he had no source. In doing so, he is again following a well-established custom that derived its authority from Thucydides. It was Thucydides' theory that it was perfectly proper to write speeches for his characters, giving the general sense of what must have been said in the style in which it must have been said. Garcilaso is following this theory when he quotes a long story from his uncle in Book I, Chapter 17 of the *Comentarios* and says in explanation, "Although I have not written it with the majesty of the words which the Inca spoke, nor with all the meaning which the words of that language have because it is so expressive, it could have been extended much more than has been done; rather I have shortened it removing some things that might make it distasteful; however it will suffice to have drawn from it the true sense of the words, which is what is appropriate to our history." The use of comparable techniques, the arrangement of events in such a fashion as to give a dramatic structure to a scene, and the introduction of emotions attributed to the characters of a history, both commonly found in Garcilaso, was a matter of dispute among historians.

Garcilaso is again in the humanistic tradition in his admiration and search for order, both in the composition of his books, and in the empires he describes. One of the purposes of insistence upon observation of chronology and geography was to give historical works a frame of order. Garcilaso frequently digresses and introduces materials outside their proper place, but he usually does so with some purpose in mind. Each of his three histories is built around a progression in time, and each of them gives the action a definite scene wherever it is possible to do so. Garcilaso's most serious complaint about his sources for the *Florida* was their carelessness in respect to time and place. He attributes many of the errors of earlier Spanish historians to their failure to observe these distinctions. He is pleased with Valera because of their shared intention to differentiate epochs and provinces in order to facilitate understanding of the customs of each group. Order in the state, based upon law, was one of the great virtues of Incan government. Besides their false religion, one of the most common reasons for the defeat of the barbarians by the Incas was their inability to establish government and to give order to their lives. It is not too much to assume that for Garcilaso one of the unfortunate results of the New Laws was the civil disorder that they aroused in the colony.

As in Bodin, whom he cites, there is in Garcilaso the suggestion of the idea of progress. The Indians progressed from a state of total barbarism to a higher state of civilization under the Incas. This state, as Garcilaso looks back upon it, has many of the qualities of the Golden Age, and its utopian character has already been remarked upon. But for all its commendable qualities, the Incan culture was seriously lacking in one aspect, that of religion. To worship the sun was better than to worship wild beasts of various kinds, but the worship of the sun was only a step toward the true religion brought by the Spaniards. Christianity was their greatest contribution to the Indians who, in accepting the faith, attained a higher degree of perfection than they had ever had before, even though it was accompanied by the loss of great wealth, power, and influence. In dividing Incan history into three parts, Garcilaso is adapting to particular circumstances a division of western history often found in the Renaissance. The first division had man living under the law of nature; the second, under the law of Moses, the third, under the law of Christ. Garcilaso did not think of progress as later generations did, but he does demonstrate that the highest state for the Indians was not to be found in the past, but in the present.

This progress that Garcilaso describes is for him the result of one of the guiding principles that give order to the universe. The whole process of human history for Garcilaso and many of his contemporaries is activated by divine providence; it is the manifestation of God's judgments and the working out of His will. Garcilaso's acceptance of this idea is another indication of the influence of Christian neo-Platonism on his thought. From the idea of the progression of the soul from the base to the divine through love of God, it is but a step to the idea of God's love extended to man, guiding him on the way to perfection.

The Renaissance was a critical, inquiring age and this aspect of his age was sympathetic to Garcilaso. He accepts and uses myth and legend in his story of the origin of the Incas; he was in fact forced to do so if he wanted to give any account at all of Manco Capac and the foundation of his empire. The charge has been made that Garcilaso was naive and gullible in his acceptance of the tales told him of the dim past. On the contrary, he displays an awareness of what those myths were and takes them, not as accurate statements of historical fact, but as containing a germ of the truth. He makes it perfectly clear that in treating of the origins of the Incas he is relating the traditions and fables handed down orally through the generations. He makes a point of reporting more than one story of the coming of Manco Capac, allowing his reader to judge the acceptability of one account over the others. Garcilaso may have believed what he was told, but he knew that he was believing legend and he knew what legend is. In the *Comentarios*, after quoting Acosta on the Incan oral compositions which related the deeds of their kings and heroes, Garcilaso comments, "Many of which the Spaniards would have to be not fables but true histories because they have some semblance of truth. They mock many others because it seems to them they are badly composed lies since they do not understand the allegory. There were many other extremely stupid ones, like some we have related." (II, 27)

Perhaps under the influence of his friends, the antiquaries and philologists Juan Fernández Franco and Ambrosio de Morales, Garcilaso makes great use of linguistic materials, especially in the *Comentarios*. It is one of his claims to authority that he knew the Indian language, was sensitive to its meanings and nuances, and was therefore in much better position to interpret what the Indians told the Spaniards. Hardly a chapter of the *Comentarios* is without some discussion of the language. He discusses the roots of words, their basic meanings and their metaphorical use, the structure of the language. He makes comparisons with Latin and Spanish; he discusses pronunciation and accentuation. For him, the full understanding of the language is the key to the interpretation of the civilization.

Along with his interest in philology, Garcilaso recognizes the value of archeological investigations. For many of the buildings destroyed by the Spaniards he searches out detailed descriptions, and at one point expresses regret that he cannot give specific dimensions.

IV Garcilaso's Authority and Influence

On the whole, Garcilaso followed the standard procedures of his age for writing history. His difference from the academic historians of Spain lies in his unconcealed personal involvement in the history he writes. It is the source both of his great success as the interpreter of Peruvian affairs, and of his failure as an historian in the eyes of his modern critics.

For many years Garcilaso was regarded in Spain and abroad as the final authority on the Incan empire; his prestige has not evaporated entirely over the centuries. Today, every historian, anthropologist, or sociologist who would study the ancient civilization of the Andes must at least consider Garcilaso's work, if only to reject it. In the seventeenth and eighteenth centuries, his claims to special knowledge and insight were generally accepted at face value. It was taken for granted that his privileged position as a connection of the royal house of the Incas and his unusual opportunities to learn about the empire had produced a history almost unique in its authority. The two parts of the *Comentarios reales* and the *Florida* were clearly the work of an intelligent, educated man, not the rough account of some untrained soldier; before he published any of his histories he had established himself as a man of learning with his translation of the *Dialoghi d'amore*. All of that added to his prestige as a trustworthy interpreter of his own people. Although it has no bearing upon the dependability of his work as history, Garcilaso's literary talents have attracted readers from his own day to this; so convincingly does he write that undoubtedly many of his less critical readers have been persuaded merely by his way with words.

It was during the eighteenth century, and in France rather than in Spain, that Garcilaso enjoyed his greatest vogue. Garcilaso had something to offer rationalists and pre-romantics alike. His description of the Indians of Peru, with their advanced civilization, their freedom from all social evils and their idyllic happiness, was highly popular because of the wide-spread concept of the noble savage. Garcilaso's Incas represented the native of America, untouched by the corrupting influence of European civilization, who managed to create a society very much like the one dreamed of by Rousseau and his associates. It was of small consequence that the Incan government imposed as many restrictions as any European government, or that the absence of crime was due to harsh laws and summary justice; what was significant was that a civilization had been developed without European influence. As soon as Europeans appeared on the scene, the picture changed, and the corruption of the original society was assured. The introduction of Christianity would not have been adequate compensation for so great a loss. The *Comentarios* and the *Historia* were proof of the theory.

With the passionate interest of the rationalists and Encyclopedists in man's social organization, the modern social sciences began to develop. Voltaire's *Essai sur les moeurs* has been considered as the foundation of cultural history as it is known today. Garcilaso offered these men considerable material, and with his detailed description of all phases of Incan civilization must be considered as a precursor of the social historians of the eighteenth century. His influence on French thought has never been given the searching analysis it deserves. When Jean François Marmontel was censured by the Sorbonne and the archbishop of Paris because of a chapter in his *Bélisaire,* he replied with *Les Incas ou la destruction de l'empire du Pérou* whose purpose was to demonstrate the dire effects of religious fanaticism among the conquerors. *Les Incas* is little more than a paraphrase of the *Comentarios reales.* Directly or indirectly, Garcilaso is supposed to have influenced the thinking of Rousseau, Fourier, and Chateaubriand. Voltaire's *Alzire,* the Abbé Raynal's *L'histoire philosophique et politique des établissements et du commerce des Européens dans les deux Indes,* and Jean Philippe Rameau's opera, *Les Indes galantes,* are all said to owe something to Garcilaso.

In Spain and Peru, Garcilaso's works attracted considerable attention at the end of the eighteenth century. In 1780, a descendant of the Inca kings, José Gabriel Condorcanqui, led a revolt of the Indians against the heavy taxation imposed by royal officials to ease the financial distress of Charles III. Under the name of Tupac Amaru II, Condorcanqui fought a bloody war against the Spaniards which lasted for three years. It is doubtful that Condorcanqui had any real hope or intention of restoring the ancient monarchy, but by taking the name of the sixteenth-century rebel, he encouraged the nervous Spaniards in the belief that his aim was to become emperor.

Charles III issued a royal order to the viceroy of Buenos Aires on April 21, 1782, in which he ignored the true cause of the rebellion and took action against what he thought was a serious contributing factor to unrest in the Andes. The first part of the order concerns the abominable practice of the *Audiencia* of Peru in allowing the Indians to refer to themselves as Incas; that practice was to cease at once because it kept alive the memory of the pre-conquest empire and was a source of inspiration for rebellion. The second item in the order concerned Garcilaso; the viceroy was ordered to remove from circulation the "History of the Inca Garcilaso where those natives have learned many harmful things." [3] The viceroy was authorized to use royal funds to purchase copies of the books, if that were the only way to remove them from circulation. Considering the financial difficulties of the Crown at this time, the willingness to expend public funds is eloquent testimony of the influence of Garcilaso.

V Reevaluation of Garcilaso's Histories

Shortly before Garcilaso's work was distinguished by its prohibition in Spain, the Scottish historian William Robertson was casting a critical eye upon the *Comentarios*, and began the modern reevaluation of Garcilaso's histories.[4] In his *History of the Discovery and Settlement of America*, Robertson acknowledged that Garcilaso enjoyed considerable prestige but implied that his reputation was inflated. His objection was that the *Comentarios* consisted largely of quotations from other historians and comment on them. He charged that it was vain to attempt to find any kind of order in the work, and that Garcilaso was incapable of distinguishing the true from the fabulous. He grudgingly admits that the *Comentarios* are of some use because of some of the Incan traditions preserved in it and because Garcilaso's knowledge of the Indian language enabled him to correct errors of others.

The attitude of the great historian, William H. Prescott, is an interesting one. In his *History of the Conquest of Peru*, Prescott depended heavily upon Garcilaso. Like Robertson, he was troubled by many of the things he found in the *Comentarios*, but he still found, as he puts it, a germ of truth in the book. A long, critical note at the end of his Book II gives a rational and balanced judgment of Garcilaso's merits and his faults. Without that note, it would be easy to conclude that Prescott entertained a very low opinion of Garcilaso; other notes reflect a certain lack of sympathy. He further remarks in a note to Chapter 2, Book V: "But it is more probable that a credulous gossip like Garcilaso should be in error than that Charles the Fifth should have been prepared to make such an acknowledgment of his imbecility . . ." Another note to Chapter 2, Book III, is not flattering to Garcilaso; ". . . the defects of his own character as an historian—his childish credulity, and his desire to magnify and mystify everything relating to his own order, and, indeed, his nation."

Since the early doubts expressed by Robertson and by Prescott, Garcilaso's work, particularly the *Comentarios reales* and the *Historia*, have been subjected to much critical scrutiny. His detractors have made much of his prejudiced point of view, and have accused him of bad faith in the omission of information essential to the complete history of the conquest of Peru. They have pointed out his numerous errors in fact, especially when he is dealing with the activities of the Spaniards. His tendency to idealize conditions, and to ignore what did not contribute to his idealization has been distasteful to many. He has been accused of plagiarism in his use of Valera's manuscripts. There have been severe criticisms for his failure to recognize the existence of a pre-Incan culture and of civilization in the provinces conquered by the Incas. His defenders, sometimes on no more solid critical ground than some of his attackers, have attempted to show that his description of Incan life and customs is accurate. His easy access to information not available to others is emphasized. Today the *Historia* is generally regarded as undependable for its factual content, and is rarely cited as authority except in matters where Garcilaso's personal participation gives him a special claim to authenticity. The *Comentarios,* on the other hand, is still used as a basic source of information on the Incas, despite the doubts that have been cast upon it. The final evaluation of his statements about the Incan civilization will have to await the results of investigations by archeologists, anthropologists, and linguists in which no preconceived notions of Garcilaso's rightness or wrongness will enter.

CHAPTER 8

Epilogue

T
HE Inca Garcilaso de la Vega is for Peruvians of today the founder of their literary tradition and the symbol of what was best in the mixture of Indian and Spanish blood. He was the first native defender of his nation, her first representative in the intellectual life of the western world.

Garcilaso's great service to his nation was in writing its history from the point of view of a true native, one who could give Europeans some idea, not only of what the Indian civilization had been, but what it had become. The history of the New World, until the appearance of Garcilaso's books, had been the work of Spaniards, and of necessity had reflected the European's attitude toward the conquered people. The *Comentarios* and the *Historia* challenged that approach and opened the way for a reevaluation of the position of the Indian and the mestizo. Garcilaso helped prepare the way for the wars of independence in the early nineteenth century with his patriotic tribute to the Indian, especially inspiring at a time when the dignity of the Indian was at its ebb. He was a precursor of the twentieth-century novelists and poets who have become aroused by the hateful condition to which the Indian has been reduced, and who have sought to restore something of his dignity.

Garcilaso refers to himself often as a humble Indian, or as a mestizo who had no claim to distinction, but in truth he was neither. He was an extraordinary man who, even without his special status and his special theme, would have left his mark on the intellectual life of Spain. Before he turned to the history of the New World, on the basis of little formal education, he made a contribution to humanistic studies in the form of his translation of the *Dialoghi d'amore*, a highly technical work that demanded considerable talent and devotion. The translation of the philosophical dialogues is all but forgotten today, but his histories are not. The *Florida*, the *Comen-*

tarios reales, and the *Historia general del Perú,* defective though they may be in many ways, have all retained a peculiar value that will never be lost. They are the reflection of an age. If they do not report with the strictest objective accuracy the events of a time already past when they were written, they do give a true account of how those events were considered, and of what they meant to the late sixteenth and early seventeenth centuries. They form a kind of spiritual autobiography of Garcilaso, whose defeats, disappointments, and frustrations were those of the people he describes.

The Inca Garcilaso found himself in a strange position. He was the son of an Indian princess of the royal family and of a noble Spanish captain, the offspring of the conquered and the conqueror. He learned the traditions and language of his mother's people at the same time that he was being exposed to the European culture of his father. As a child, he was more intimately associated with his mother and her tradition; as a youth, he turned toward his father's people; as a mature man, he took his place in Spain among his Spanish relatives. In the end, in spite of his mixed heritage, he identified himself with European culture, although he could never lose the emotional ties to his childhood. He was torn between his sympathetic, romantic attachment to an Indian tradition destroyed by European power and his wish to become a part of that destructive power. He was both the victor and the vanquished, the master and the slave, the oppressor and the victim.

Notes and References

Preface

1. Marcelino Menéndez y Pelayo's opinion of Garcilaso is expressed in *Historia de la poesía hispano-americana*, ed. Enrique Sánchez Reyes (Santander, 1948), II, 76–77.

Chapter One

1. Still the best and most detailed account of the Spanish conquest of Peru is William H. Prescott's *History of the Conquest of Peru*, first published in 1847. It is available in many editions, among them that of the Modern Library.

Chapter Two

1. Details of the genealogy of the Inca Garcilaso are to be found in several sources, among them, Aurelio Miró Quesada y Sosa, *El Inca Garcilaso* (Madrid, 1948), pp. 7–21.
2. The life of Garcilaso in Cuzco is drawn from his works, principally the *Florida del Inca*, I, 2; II¹, 1, 27; VI, 2; *Comentarios reales*, I, 1, 15, 19; II, 4, 26, 27; III, 1, 16, 23; IV, 20; V, 2, 5, 27, 29; VI, 7, 9, 24, 28; VII, 7, 8, 11, 21, 29; VIII, 16, 24, 25; IX, 16, 17, 18, 24, 25, 37, 38; *Historia general del Perú, Prólogo;* I, 2, 32; II, 25, 27; III, 19; IV, 9, 10, 21, 42; V, 2, 3, 6, 8, 10, 25, 27, 39, 42; VI, 1, 3, 6; VII, 12, 20, 22, 24, 25; VIII, 1, 2, 11, 18.

Additional information of Garcilaso's parents is to be found in Miró Quesada, *El Inca Garcilaso*, pp. 42–77; the will of Garcilaso's mother is reproduced on pp. 250–53. His father's will may be found in Carlos Daniel Valcárcel Esparza, *Garcilazo Inka* (Lima, 1939), pp. 45–48.

3. The letter quoted is one of two written by Garcilaso to Juan Fernández Franco, published in Eugenio Asensio, "Dos cartas desconocidas del Inca Garcilaso," *Nueva Revista de Filología Hispánica*, VII (1954), 583–89.
4. Most of the material in this section depends heavily upon the preliminary essay and the documents published in Raúl Porras Barrenechea, *El Inca Garcilaso en Montilla, 1561–1614* (Lima, 1955). This valuable book also contains a section on Cervantes and La Camacha, "Cervantes, la Camacha y Montilla," pp. 230–50.
5. The quotation concerning Alonso de Vargas and the subsequent information on Garcilaso's dealings with the Marquesas de Priego come from "Relación de la descendencia de Garci Pérez de Vargas," which remained unpublished in Garcilaso's lifetime, and which was apparently intended originally to serve as a prologue to the *Florida*. It is to be found in the *Obras completas del Inca Garcilaso de la Vega*, ed. Carmelo Sáenz de Santa María (Madrid, 1960), I, 229–40.
6. Documents of Garcilaso's appointment as captain are in Guillermo Lohmann Villena, "Apostillas documentales en torno al Inca Garcilaso," *Mercurio Peruano*, no. 375 (julio, 1958).
7. The interpretation of Garcilaso's attitude toward his poverty was expressed by José Durand in his comments during a symposium on Garcilaso held in Lima, June 17–28, 1955. The proceedings are published in *Nuevos estudios sobre el Inca Garcilaso de la Vega* (Lima, 1955). Professor Durand's remarks are found on pp. 56–59.

8. Garcilaso's copy of Las Casas' treatises is described in Rubén Vargas Ugarte, "Nota sobre Garcilaso," *Mercurio Peruano*, nos. 137–138 (1930).
9. The identity of Diego de Vargas is discussed in Rafael Aguilar y Priego, "El hijo del Inca Garcilaso. Nuevos documentos sobre Diego de Vargas," *Boletín de la Real Academia de Córdoba*, XXI (1950), 45–48.
10. Documentary sources for the life of Garcilaso in Córdoba are found in José de la Torre y del Cerro, *El Inca Garcilaso de la Vega. Neuva documentación* (Madrid, 1935).
11. The contents of Garcilaso's library are identified and analyzed in José Durand, "La biblioteca del Inca," *Nueva Revista de Filología Hispánica*, II (1948), 239–64.
12. Garcilaso's relations with Fernández de Córdoba and Aldrete are discussed in José Durand, "Dos notas sobre el Inca Garcilaso," *Nueva Revista de Filología Hispánica*, III (1949), 278–90.

Chapter Three

1. The correspondence with Maximiliano de Austria and the letters to the King form a part of the preliminary documents to the *Diálogos de amor*. They are published in *Obras completas*, I, 3–13.
2. For discussion of Hebreo's *Dialoghi d'amore* and the Renaissance neo-Platonic doctrine of love, see John Charles Nelson, *Renaissance Theory of Love* (New York, 1958), Chapter II, "Love Treatises," and Nesca A. Robb, *Neoplatonism of the Italian Renaissance* (London, 1935), Chapter VI, "The Trattato d'Amore."

Chapter Four

1. Julia Fitzmaurice Kelley in her *The Inca Garcilaso* (Oxford, 1921) identified Silvestre as the probable source for the *Florida*, basing her opinion largely on internal evidence.

2. A detailed account of the career of Silvestre is found in Aurelio Miró Quesada's "Prólogo" to *La Florida del Inca*, ed. Emma Susana Speratti Piñero (Mexico, 1956).
3. The memorial regarding Silvestre's debt is published in de la Torre y del Cerro, document no. 129.
4. The Portuguese title of the book by the "Gentleman of Elvas" is: *Relaçam verdadeira dos trabalhos que ho gobernador dom Fernando de Souto e certos fidalgos portugueses passaron no descobrimiento da provincia de Florida. Agora novamente feita per hun fidalgo Delvas.*
5. Miró Quesada's discussion of Garcilaso's debt to the romances of chivalry will be found in his *El Inca Garcilaso*, pp. 140–41.

Chapter Six

1. Views on Viceroy Toledo differing from those of Garcilaso are found in Arthur Franklin Zimmerman, *Francisco de Toledo, Fifth Viceroy of Peru 1569–1581* (Caldwell, Idaho, 1938) and in Roberto Levillier, *Don Francisco de Toledo, supremo organizador del Perú*, 3 vols. (Madrid, Buenos Aires, 1935–1942).

Chapter Seven

1. For a history of Renaissance historiography, see Éduard Fueter, *Histoire de l'historiographie moderne*, trans. Emile Jaumarie (Paris, 1914).
2. Cicero's views on history are found in his *De oratore*, Book II.
3. The royal order recalling copies of Garcilaso's works may be read in Luis A. Arocena, *El Inca Garcilaso y el humanismo renacentista* (Buenos Aires, 1949), pp. 68–69.
4. William Robertson's evaluation of Garcilaso is in his *The History of the Discovery and Settlement of America*, note 125. The book was first published in 1777; it is available in many editions.

Selected Bibliography

PRIMARY SOURCES

Principal Editions of the Works of Garcilaso
1. *Complete works*
Obras completas del Inca Garcilaso de la Vega, ed. Carmelo Sáenz de Santa María. 4 vols. Madrid: Ediciones Atlas, 1960. (Vols. 132–135 of the *Biblioteca de Autores Españoles.*)
2. *Diálogos de amor*
La traduzion del Indio de los tres Dialogos de Amor de Leon Hebreo, hecha de Italiano en Español por Garcilasso Inga de la Vega, natural de la gran Ciudad del Cuzco, cabeza de los Reynos y Porvincias del Piru. (Madrid: En casa de Pedro Madrigal, 1590.) First edition.
Hebreo, León. *Diálogos de amor traducidos por Garcilaso Inga de la Vega,* ed. Eduardo Juliá Martínez. 2 vols. (Madrid: Librería General Victoriano Suárez, 1949.)
3. *La Florida del Inca*
La Florida del Ynca. Historia del Adelantado Hernando de Soto, Gouernador y capitan general del Reyno de la Florida y de otros heroicos caualleros Españoles e Yndios; escrita por el Ynca Garcilasso de la Vega, capitan de su Magestad, natural de la gran ciudad del Cozco, cabeza de los Reynos y provincias del Peru. (Lisbona: Impresso por Pedro Crasbeeck, 1605.) First edition.
La Florida del Inca. (Madrid: N. Rodríguez Franco, 1723.)
La Florida del Inca, ed. Emma Susana Speratti Piñero. Prólogo de Aurelio Miró Quesada. Estudio bibliográfico de José Durand. (México: Fonda de Cultura Económica, 1956.)
4. *Comentarios reales*
Primera parte de los Comentarios Reales que tratan del origen de los Yncas, reyes que fueron del Peru, de su idolatria, leyes, y govierno en paz y en guerra: de sus vidas y conquistas, y de todo lo que fue aquel imperio y su republica antes que los españoles passaran a el. Escritos por el Ynca Garcilasso de la Vega, natural del Cozco y capitan de Su Majestad. (Lisboa: En la Officina de Pedro Crasbeeck. 1609.) First edition.
Primera parte de los Comentarios Reales. (Madrid: Oficina Real, y a costa de Nicolas Rodriguez Franco, 1723.)
Comentarios reales de los Incas, ed. Angel Rosenblat. 2 vols. (Buenos Aires: Emecé Editores, S.A., 1943.)
5. Historia general del Perú
Historia General del Peru. Trata el descubrimiento del; y como lo ganaron los españoles. Las guerras civiles que hubo entre Pizarros y Almagros, sobre la partija de la tierra. Castigo y levantamiento de tiranos: y otros sucesos particulares que en la historia se contienen. Escrita por el Ynca Garcilasso de la Vega, Capitan de su majestad, etc. (Cordoba: Por la Viuda de Andres Barrera. 1617.) First edition.
Historia general del Perú. (Madrid: Oficina Real, y a costa de Nicolas Rodriguez Franco, 1722.)
Historia general del Perú (Segunda parte de los Comentarios reales de los Incas), ed. Angel Rosenblat. 3 vols. (Buenos Aires: Emecé Editores, S. A., 1944.)
6. *English translations*
The Florida of the Inca. Translated by John Grier Varner and Jeannette Johnson Varner. (Austin: University of Texas Press, 1951.)
The Royal Commentaries of Peru in two parts . . . rendered into English

by Sir Paul Rycaut. (London: Printed by M. Flesher for S. Heyrick, 1688.) A translation of both parts of the *Comentarios* into English; very freely rendered and full of errors.

First Part of the Royal Commentaries of the Yncas. Translated with notes and an introduction by Sir Clements R. Markham. 2 vols. (London: Printed for the Hakluyt Society, 1869–1871). Hakluyt Society *Works*, vols. XLI, XLV. A complete modern translation into English of the *Comentarios reales.*

Royal Commentaries of the Incas and General History of Peru. Translated with an introduction by Harold V. Livermore. Foreword by Arnold J. Toynbee. 2 vols. (Austin and London: University of Texas Press, 1966.) The only complete modern translation into English of both parts of the *Comentarios reales.*

The Incas. The Royal Commentaries of the Inca Garcilaso de la Vega. Translated by Maria Jolas. Introduction by Alain Gheerbrant. (New York: Orion Press, 1961.) Also available in paperback edition of Avon Books. A badly cut version of the *Comentarios reales* which gives a distorted view of the work. A tenth book has been added, drawn from the first book of the *Historia general del Perú.*

SECONDARY SOURCES

A complete bibliography on Garcilaso is contained in *Obras completas,* I, lxviii–lxxvii.

AROCENA, LUIS A. *El Inca Garcilaso y el humanismo renacentista.* (Buenos Aires: Centro de Profesores Diplomados de Enseñanza Secundaria, 1949.) A well documented study which relates Garcilaso to the humanist tradition in Europe.

FITZMAURICE KELLEY, JULIA. *The Inca Garcilaso.* (Oxford: Oxford University Press, 1921.) The only general work on Garcilaso in English, now outdated because of information discovered since its publication.

MIRÓ QUESADA Y SOSA, AURELIO. *El Inca Garcilaso.* (Madrid: Instituto de Cultura Hispánica, 1948.) The best general treatment of the life and works of Garcilaso.

Nuevos estudios sobre el Inca Garcilaso de la Vega. Actas del symposium realizado en Lima del 17 al 28 de junio de 1955. (Lima: Banco crédito del Perú, 1955.) An interesting and valuable collection of papers with comments on them by Peru's leading Garcilaso scholars; many phases of the life and works of Garcilaso are discussed.

PORRAS BARRENECHEA, RAÚL. *El Inca Garcilaso en Montilla, 1561–1614.* (Lima: Editorial San Marcos, 1955.) Essential for the biography of Garcilaso during his stay in Montilla because of the archival documents reproduced.

SÁNCHEZ, LUIS ALBERTO. *Garcilaso Inca de la Vega. Primer criollo.* (Santiago de Chile; Ediciones Ercilla, 1939.) A poetic account of the life of Garcilaso, lacking in documentation.

DE LA TORRE Y DEL CERRO, JOSÉ. *El Inca Garcilaso de la Vega. Nueva documentación.* (Madrid: Impr. de J. Murillo, 1935.) An indispensable collection of documents covering Garcilaso's residence in Córdoba.

VALCÁRCEL, LUIS E. *Garcilaso el Inca.* (Lima, Imprenta del Museo Nacional, 1939). The thesis here is that Garcilaso was influenced but little, if at all, by Spanish culture; he is motivated almost entirely by his Indian heritage.

VALCÁRCEL ESPARZA, CARLOS DANIEL. *Garcilazo Inka.* (Lima, E. Bustamante y Ballirián, 1939). A work that seems to lack direction in spite of its subtitle, "Ensayo sico-histórico," but which has some useful suggestions.

Index

Index

73970

868.3
C346

DATE DUE

GAYLORD | | | PRINTED IN U.S.A.